THEY **DRANK**
FROM THE RIVER
AND **DIED** IN
THE WILDERNESS

THEY **DRANK**

FROM THE RIVER
AND **DIED** IN
THE WILDERNESS

DAVID RAVENHILL

Destiny Image₍ᵣ₎ Publishers, Inc.
P.O. Box 310
Shippensburg, PA 17257-0310

"Speaking to the Purposes of God for This Generation
and for the Generations to Come"

ISBN 0-7684-2038-5

For Worldwide Distribution
Printed in the U.S.A.

First Printing: 2000   Second Printing: 2000

This book and all other Destiny Image, Revival Press, MercyPlace, Fresh Bread, and Treasure House books are available at Christian bookstores and distributors worldwide.

For a U.S. bookstore nearest you, call **1-800-722-6774**.
For more information on foreign distributors, call **717-532-3040**.
Or reach us on the Internet: **http://www.reapernet.com**

Dedication

Every writer comes by truth through a variety of ways.
There is revelation which comes
by way of contemplation and meditation.
Truth also comes through instruction, observation,
participation and investigation.
Over the years I have gleaned from all of these sources.
I am profoundly grateful to God as well as His
numerous servants who have
so richly contributed to my spiritual knowledge
and understanding.
What you are about to read is in a large part due to the impact
that others have made upon my life.
I have listened, observed and read not only their writings
but more importantly their lives.
To all those many saints
who have helped fashion my life
as well as instill in me a hunger for God
I gratefully dedicate this book.

Endorsements

This is an important book! I urge everyone who has been involved in any of the current renewal and revival movements to carefully digest the prophetic warnings and prayerful wisdom contained in these pages. It could save you from being shipwrecked in the river!

Dr. Michael L. Brown
President, Brownsville Revival School of Ministry

Like a scorching hot branding iron, David Ravenhill burns the mark of the cross of Christ Jesus upon you through the convicting and cutting words of this timely book. Want to go deeper and farther in the "river of God's purposes" in this hour? Then do what this book teaches!

Jim W. Goll
Ministry to the Nations
Author of *The Lost Art of Intercession*,
and *Father, Forgive Us!*

I believe the true test of a revival is ten years later. David Ravenhill, who lives with a God-given, burning desire for true revival, is extremely concerned over the present move of God. He is not afraid to ask probing questions. This book, *They Drank From the River and Died in the Wilderness*, is right on time.

David's writings cut like a surgeon's knife. Through the pages of this book, the reader will quickly discover that God is not out to hurt—but to heal. If you have grown lazy, you will be startled awake. For those who have grown lukewarm, David's words will be used of God to stoke the smoldering embers. He gleans from Holy Scripture the mistakes of the past, and warns God's people not to succumb to the same seductions.

The church today needs the voice of David Ravenhill. My friend, this book will challenge your soul and charge your spirit.

Stephen Hill
Evangelist

A timely reminder that a plunge into the "river" is not enough; we must learn to swim as well.

Dr. R.T. Kendall
Westminster Chapel
London

Like his father, Leonard, David Ravenhill has a distinct call concerning revival. I eagerly await any new material he releases because it is so fresh—it is cutting edge, and full of scholarly wisdom. The emerging awakened Church of the twenty-first century should adopt this as a handbook. It's a masterpiece.

John A. Kilpatrick
Senior Pastor, Brownsville Assembly of God
Pensacola, Florida

Contents

Prologue

The Enemy's "River" of Deception

THE Word of God consistently uses the analogy of rivers to describe the ministry and work of the Holy Spirit. Therefore, it stands to reason that the enemy would seek to counterfeit the river of God and thereby undermine God's plan and purpose for His Church.

Revelation 12 tells us that the devil is seeking to devour the man child that is to be born. Following this, we are told, the devil will pour forth a river from his mouth in order to sweep away or destroy the woman (the Church). I believe that we need to give this passage some serious consideration because of the destructive nature of this "event." Everything God does, the enemy seeks to capitalize upon for his own purposes. The devil's greatest weapon is deception. Jesus repeatedly warned His disciples that these last days would be marked by a deception so subtle and clever that, if possible, it would deceive the very elect. In fact, the devil's strategy includes deceiving people into thinking that it will come in the form of some New Age type of teaching and that any reasonably mature believer will see it coming a mile away.

A careful study of God's Word reveals that deception involves far more than denying the virgin birth, the atonement, or another basic tenet of the faith. Nor does it simply mean to be carried away by "mantras and crystals" or some other New Age phenomenon.

Deception first begins with this attitude: "I cannot be deceived." However, consider the words of Obadiah: "The pride of your heart has deceived you" (verse 3, NIV); or Jeremiah's words: "The heart is deceitful above all things, and desperately wicked: who can know it?" (17:9 KJV) It's the little foxes that spoil the vines and the little leaven that eventually affects everything.

I suggest that you look at some of the verses dealing with deception and honestly ask yourself, "How well am I doing in resisting the deception and devices of the enemy?"

Paul warns the Galatians not to think that they can sow yet not reap the consequences of their actions: "Be not deceived...whatsoever a man soweth, that shall he also reap" (6:7 KJV). Recently I received a phone call from the wife of a prominent songwriter and recording artist. She said that her husband, who continues to travel a lot, has been involved in numerous immoral situations with the wives of some of his friends. Is this man deceived? I believe so.

This situation is a prime example of the deception Paul warns the Corinthians about: "Do not be deceived, neither fornicators, nor idolaters, nor adulterers...shall inherit the kingdom of God" (1 Cor. 6:9a-10). How many falsely assume that they will not reap the result of their actions and that they can still participate in God's Kingdom and calling?

One of the great blessings of the river of God is its liberating power. It has freed thousands from the bondage of legalism and religion and brought them into the glorious liberty of the sons of God. However, there is a fine line between Holy Ghost liberty and carnal freedom.

Paul deals with another deception in his letter to the Galatians when he admonishes, "If anyone thinks he is something when he is nothing, he deceives himself" (6:3 NIV). The old Puritans had a saying that pride is the last thing to leave the human heart and the first thing to return. How readily we buy into the deception that "we are something" and therefore superior to everyone else.

Once while in Malaysia and Singapore for a time of ministry, I was told on two separate occasions of how well-known international ministries had been through these centers, but had left behind them the reputation of being arrogant, ungrateful, and aloof. Why is it that these "servants of God" insist that they be flown first class, put up in the finest hotels, and paid the wage of some superstars? Whatever happened to integrity, humility, and accessibility? Unfortunately, when we buy into the belief that we are "something," it isn't too long before we start believing that we should be pampered with whatever it is that makes us—including our flesh and carnal nature—feel good.

James warns about yet another area of deception: "If anyone considers himself religious and yet does not keep a tight rein on his tongue, he deceives himself..." (1:26 NIV). How readily we assume that we are spiritual simply because we think we are. Unfortunately, our mouth betrays us. James also mentions what possibly might be one of the greatest deceptions in the Church when he says, "Prove yourselves doers of the word, and not merely hearers who delude [deceive] themselves" (1:22). Talk is cheap. Backing words with a life of obedience is a true measure of a man or woman of God.

One of the more recent fads among God's people is wearing ornaments and clothing that flash the letters WWJD, or "What Would Jesus Do?" It's one thing to thunder this popular phrase from the pulpit, but it is quite another thing to put it into practice in daily living. "What would Jesus do" applies to more than just sin; it applies to our whole manner of life. One of my pet peeves is receiving shocked surprise from small congregations when I tell them that I am happy to come and minister for them. Why is it that once a man of God becomes popular, he is no longer able to minister in small settings, but rather restricts his ministry to the big churches and to the ever-increasing conference circuit? I seem to remember reading somewhere that Jesus fulfilled His Father's purpose by ministering to the woman at the well as much as by ministering to the 5,000. But maybe that was another Jesus!

Now that I have your attention on how easily we can be deceived, let's consider again the enemy's ability to deceive us. Today's move of God has a number of issues that need to be addressed. Jesus warned His disciples in Matthew that when the floods come, they will test the quality of each man's house. You will recall that it was only the house that was built on the rock that survived the flood. Let me remind you again that in Revelation 12 the serpent poured water like a river out of his mouth after the woman, in order to cause her to be swept away with the flood. In Matthew's Gospel Jesus described how the man who built his house on the sand lost everything because of the flood. Now consider this interesting observation from *Merriam-Webster's Collegiate Dictionary*: Sand is defined as "a loose granular material that results from the disintegration of rock."[1]

What does this mean? One of my great concerns with regard to this present outpouring is the increasing tendency to build upon "sand" rather than upon the rock of God's Word. How readily we grasp at loose grains of truth rather than the whole rock! As a teacher, I am concerned that we are producing a generation of believers hooked on experiences rather than exposition. We get more excited over some feelings than we do over God's Word. People flock to see some demonstration of God's power, but they run from any desire to know the person of God Himself. We now give more emphasis to praise than we do to prayer, and possessions have replaced passion and purity. Success is no longer measured by character, but by charisma. Gifting has replaced godliness. Put on a gospel concert, and you can fill most auditoriums. Call people to pray, and you can fit them into the smallest room of the church.

I feel that we are in danger of being swept away by the enemy's river of deception. Thousands line up to experience "holy laughter," but few make the transition to "holy living." Others swarm to hear about financial prosperity, but know little of spiritual prosperity.

Finally, I am reminded of James' statement, "Let not many of you become teachers...knowing that as such we shall incur a stricter judgment" (3:1). Spiritual leaders of God's people have an awesome responsibility to build according to the pattern. I would like to issue a challenge to the leaders of this move to take time out in order to reassess where we are going. I believe that it is time for some honest talking and discussion. When Manoah (Samson's father) was informed by his wife that she was about to have a child, he begged God to allow the angel to return and instruct him on how the child was to be raised. God has seen fit to give us a "child." We now need the wisdom of God on how to raise it for God's ultimate glory and purpose. Let's seek to know how to make the transition from *privilege* to *purpose*.

ENDNOTE

1. *Merriam-Webster's Collegiate Dictionary*, 10th ed. (Springfield, Massachusetts: Merriam-Webster, Inc., 1996), "sand."

Foreword

DAVID RAVENHILL strikes at the root of the problem when he tells us that "Deception first begins with this attitude: 'I cannot be deceived.' " His admonition to finish well may not be as exciting as the burning rubber of a tire-squealing start—but finishing well is far more important than simply starting well. How many Christians have "DNF" written by their name in heaven—*Did Not Finish!* They came close—close enough to drink, close enough to play, close enough to get wet...yet never crossed. The mature value finishing the race. Both Mary of the alabaster box and Judas of the 30 pieces of silver kissed Jesus—but one did not finish well. How tragic to kiss the door of heaven and wind up in hell. I want to drink and not die—let me cross! Let me finish well!

Don't feel that David Ravenhill is attacking the "river" (or the church, renewal or revival). He affirms its divine origins and purpose. *There's nothing wrong with the river!* But it's not meant to camp by—we must cross over! Jordan can be a barrier or a protective border—it just depends on which side you're on! *Cross over—you can drink just as well from the other side!*

Move from the place of *privilege* to the place of *purpose*, from the people of God *among* the nations, to the priests of God *to* the nations. The river is not the goal! It's a "gate"! Cross and enter—God's promises are in the promised land! Wildness is in the wilderness! The wilderness is only the *bridge* between slavery and sonship—Egypt and Canaan. Don't die en route!

With this book David Ravenhill takes his rightful place as a voice to the body, just as his father was. To grow up in the shadow of a famous father like Leonard Ravenhill carries its own baggage. David has done so with grace, but he is no longer in the shadow. The anointing and mantle that was on his father now rests comfortably on his shoulders.

I suspect that Leonard Ravenhill and his friend A.W. Tozer are smiling from the balconies of Heaven. This book sounds and smells like their works, and will impact you the same way. David Ravenhill has captured timeless truths in contemporary context. This book could well become a classic—read it now, and keep your prayer mat nearby...you may need to kneel!

Tommy Tenney
Author and Godchaser

Introduction

THE book you are holding never would have been written had it not been for a divine appointment—one of those rare times when the Spirit of God speaks to you and you cannot deny it.

I had just completed some meetings with a combined group of churches in Carlsbad, New Mexico, and was on my way to a conference in northern California. I had had one free day before the conference began, until a local church in the area found out and contacted me to see if I would minister at one of their renewal meetings. I had agreed. So needless to say, I was already tired when, three flights later, I arrived in Sacramento. When I arrived at the church, I was given the option of spending some time alone in the pastor's office or joining the pre-service prayer time. I opted to be alone. What happened next is the reason this book was written.

As I sat there in the office, I began to meditate upon the "rivers" in God's Word. My thoughts began at the first river, the river God had caused to flow out of the first tabernacle: the Garden of Eden. Flowing forth from the very presence of God was a river that divided and became four great rivers. These "rivers of life" had their origin in the dwelling place of God Himself.

I then began thinking of Ezekiel's great vision of the river that flowed from under the altar of the temple. As the water flowed forth, it became deeper and deeper and more and more majestic. This mighty torrent of water brought life to every place it flowed. The landscape was transformed by its life-giving flow. This brought me to John's description of the final river we find in God's Word, found in Revelation 22. John was shown a river—a river full of the water of life, clear as crystal, which flowed directly from the throne of God and of the Lamb. As I was musing on these rivers, the Holy Spirit simply said, "What about First Corinthians 10?" Suddenly, I found myself quoting this passage: "[They] all ate the same spiritual food; and all drank the same spiritual drink, for they were drinking from a spiritual rock which followed them; and the rock was Christ. Nevertheless with most of them God was not well-pleased; for they were laid low in the wilderness" (verses 3-5). It was then that I heard the Holy Spirit say, "They drank from the river...and died in the wilderness!" I was stunned. I sat there suddenly conscious of the fact that God was not nearly as excited about "the river" as I was. In that brief moment, I clearly understood that God's purpose for His people was far greater than "the river" alone. Now, contrary to what this book may imply, this text is not against what God is doing around the world today, which is commonly referred to as "the river."

I have spent the last two years of my ministry working throughout the United States and overseas teaching and proclaiming that God is both refreshing and renewing His people. I am not, however, prepared to declare that this is all God is doing or desiring for the Church. I believe that we are making a serious mistake if we "camp around" "the river." First Corinthians 10 is not only Paul's instruction to the local church in Corinth; it is also a prophetic warning for our generation "upon whom the ends of the ages have come" (1 Cor. 10:11).

I have become increasingly aware that we can drink from the river and yet never experience the fullness of God's purpose. It staggers me to think that between one and three million Israelites drank from the river of God's provision, yet only two made it into the Promised Land. Paul likens their and our journey to a race—a race that we all run but few finish. May God grant you the grace to persevere and the passion to run. "Drink" all you can along the way. Don't allow spiritual dehydration to sap your energy and rob you of your vitality. Keep your eyes set on the goal—and "run in such a way that you may win" (1 Cor. 9:24b).

Chapter One

Shooting Stars

NOTHING is more spectacular than a "shooting star." For countless generations people have turned their eyes skyward, gazing in amazement at the vastness of God's handiwork. On a clear night you can view the myriad of stars that make up the Milky Way. Sparkling like polished diamonds, they take your breath away with their beauty.

As you gaze upon this endless sight, suddenly a meteorite or shooting star speeds across the faraway vistas. Mesmerized by its speed and brilliance, this unusual phenomenon captivates you, drawing your attention away from the other stars. With rapt gaze you watch this comet streaking across the heavens as if shot from a cannon. No sooner does it appear, though, than it vanishes—to become a memory that you muse on momentarily.

Astronomers tell us that thousands of these "stars" are seen annually. They no doubt thrill the hearts of those who catch a glimpse of them, but they have no value whatever to those who still use the heavens for navigation. For thousands of years, sailors have charted their course by the stars. These halogen headlights of the heavens have guided many a ship to its destination, all due to their unchanging positions and constant candescence.

Years ago I heard Bob Mumford use the term "shooting stars" to refer to a type of ministry in the Body of Christ. These seemingly anointed ministries appear as if out of nowhere and within months are the talk of the Church. People flock to crusades, buy every tape and video they can afford, and follow the ministry's every move like some spiritual Pentecostal pied piper. All too tragically, these ministries soon peter out, leaving behind them disillusionment, disappointment, and confusion.

Like so many before them, these often gifted ministries fall into immorality, financial impropriety, or pride, which results in bringing God's opposition. If there is a lesson to be learned from shooting stars, it is that *how we begin is not nearly as important as how we finish.* Longevity is the critical thing. Starting off well means little in the end if we quit along the way.

STAYING THE COURSE

What is the key to longevity in Christian living and effective ministry? In a word, it is *self-control.* Self-control is essential to any successful endeavor. The apostle Paul recognized its importance as a spiritual quality. He closed his list of the fruit of the Spirit with it (see Gal. 5:22-23), indicating that self-control was the result of the workings of the rest of the fruit in a person's life. Paul majored on self-control in his first letter to the church in Corinth because they were sorely lacking in it. Here was a church of great giftedness, power, privilege, and promise, yet they were in danger of throwing it all away because they could not control their physical, spiritual, and moral appetites.

Paul addressed the problem by using one of his favorite metaphors for the Christian life: running a race.

> *Do you not know that those who run in a race all run, but only one receives the prize? Run in such a way that you may win. And everyone who competes in the games exercises self-control in all things. They then do it to receive a perishable wreath, but we an imperishable. Therefore I run in such a way, as not without aim; I box in such a way, as not beating the air; but I buffet my body and make it my slave, lest possibly, after I have preached to others, I myself should be disqualified* (1 Corinthians 9:24-27).

Paul states that *all* believers are in a race—he's in a race, the Corinthians are in a race, and we who are believers at the dawn of the third millennium are in a race. We are to run in such a way as to win. Anyone who has any hope or dream of winning, lives and trains with the prize in mind. That is self-control: discipline, restraint, self-denial. Now, Paul doesn't call on others to do what he is unwilling to do himself. Indeed, he says, "I run...as not without aim...I buffet my body and make it my slave." Paul was unyielding in the discipline and self-control that he required of himself. Why? If he had done anything less, he would have run the risk of not completing the race—of stumbling and falling before reaching the finish line.

Paul then reminds the Corinthians of Israel's failure in the wilderness—how they began triumphantly but ended tragically. Using Israel as an example, Paul issues a warning to the Corinthians—and to us—lest we follow the same path. He writes, "Now these things happened as examples for us....they were written for our instruction, upon whom the ends of the ages have come" (1 Cor. 10:6,11). What Paul means is that everything that happened to the nation of Israel in the wilderness has relevance for us today. To nail home the point he says, "Therefore let him who thinks he stands take heed lest he fall" (1 Cor. 10:12). In other words, "Don't think this doesn't apply to you. Don't get overconfident. If you bask in your own abilities and your own self-sufficiency, you will fall just as Israel did."

Paul is talking about the fact that *how we finish is more important than how we begin*. It's possible to have a sensational beginning and a suicidal ending. What counts is being at the finish line when the race is over, to be still standing at the end of the battle. When Ben-hadad, king of Aram, besieged Samaria, the capital city of the northern kingdom of Israel, he boasted of how he would overcome Israel. In defiance Ahab, king of Israel, responded, "Let not him who girds on his armor boast like him who takes it off" (1 Kings 20:11b). In other words, don't brag until after the battle. The one who lives to take off his armor is the true winner.

The same is true in our spiritual life. How we live along the way is important, but our lifestyle should look to the goal, the prize, the victory. We need to live for the long run, not the short haul. Otherwise, we will be shooting stars that burn out before the end. Using Paul's analogy, the Christian life is a marathon, not a sprint. That is why self-control is so vital.

A RIVER IN THE DESERT

So we are all in a race, and we must exercise self-control in all things if we are to finish victoriously. According to Paul, the nation of Israel is also in this race. In Moses' time Israel began the race well, but failed to finish.

For I do not want you to be unaware, brethren, that our fathers were all under the cloud, and all passed through the sea; and all were baptized into Moses in the cloud and in the sea; and all ate the same spiritual food; and all drank the same spiritual drink, for they were drinking from a spiritual rock which followed them; and the rock was Christ. Nevertheless, with most of them God was not well-pleased; for they were laid low in the wilderness. Now these things happened as examples for us, that we should not crave evil things, as they also craved (1 Corinthians 10:1-6).

Notice that *all* the Israelites began the race. Under God's direction and Moses' leadership they *all* were under the cloud of God's protection; they *all* passed through the sea of deliverance; they *all* enjoyed the manna provided by God for their nourishment; and they *all* drank from the river that sprang from the rock in the desert (see Ex. 17:6). Paul calls this food and drink *spiritual* because God supernaturally provided them. The "spiritual rock" that followed them and from which they drank Paul identifies as Christ Himself. The Lord was their spiritual sustenance. Yet, in spite of all this, the Israelites "were laid low in the wilderness" (1 Cor. 10:5). Out of that vast privileged population, only two—Joshua and Caleb—lived to enter God's purpose of the Promised Land.

Paul's warning is clear: Despite a great river of divine blessing and provision, the nation of Israel failed to finish the race. *They drank from the river and died in the wilderness*. The reason? Lack of self-control. Paul says that they craved "evil things" and warns us against doing the same, lest we come to a similar end. Israel's failure should be a cautionary example for us so that we might finish what they failed to complete.

THE RIVER IS HERE

How does this apply to the Church today? Just as with Israel in the wilderness, a great river of God is flowing today from which the Church is drinking abundantly. It is a river of renewal and refreshing, of healing and deliverance, of joy and laughter, of restored purpose and power. This current move of God has transformed tens of thousands of lives all over the world— strengthening marriages, bringing backsliders back into a vital relationship with the Lord, drawing thousands of lost people to a saving faith in Christ, and strengthening and encouraging churches.

Those who have experienced this "river" agree: The "river" is great. Receiving a fresh touch from God is a wonderful experience. However, as wonderful as it is, if we seek the experience, the blessing of the "river," for its own sake alone, we run the risk of failing to enter into God's full purpose for us just like the nation of Israel. With this in mind, I think it is important that we understand a few things about the river that sustained the nation of Israel in the desert. There are lessons in it for us today.

First of all, *there was nothing wrong with the river itself*. It was God's divine provision for His people; He planned and provided it. Paul also makes this clear when he identifies the source of the river as a "spiritual rock," which was Christ. *The river was divine in origin and holy in purpose.* So it is today. The Lord has freely poured out on His people a divine river of refreshing and renewal designed to bring the Church into the full purposes of God. The river is a good thing, a vital thing for the Church today. The river has broken the spiritual drought over the land, and we are seeing new life springing up across the nation.

There is a danger, though. It is the danger that every generation faces when it experiences the power of God. The danger is in becoming obsessed with the peripherals of the experience and never moving forward toward the purpose of the Eternal.

Secondly, *the river was a source of life* for the Israelites in the barren wilderness. It had to sustain a company of up to three million people, plus several million sheep, oxen, cattle, and donkeys—all of whom needed water. So this river was more than a tiny trickle issuing from a small crack in a rock; it was a veritable flood. The Psalmist described God's provision this way: "He split the rocks in the wilderness, and gave them abundant drink like the ocean depths. He brought forth streams also from the rock, and caused waters to run down like rivers" (Ps. 78:15-16). It was a considerable amount of water, equivalent to the supply needed for meeting the daily requirements of a city the size of Chicago.

The river was natural water with a spiritual origin. The lesson God wanted the Israelites to learn was that they derived their life from Him alone. In the same way, our life is derived from the Rock, Jesus Christ. Just as Moses, under God's direction, struck the rock and water poured forth for the people, so Jesus was stricken on the cross and from His bruised body and shed blood poured *our* life.

God always does things lavishly, doesn't He? With Him there are no halfway measures. When Jesus fed the multitude, He didn't simply give them a snack to take the edge off their hunger; instead, He fed them so that "they all ate, and were satisfied" (Mt. 14:20). In fact, afterwards the disciples gathered up 12 baskets full of leftovers! God never does things in a minor way. He wants to satisfy us fully. When we ask for a cup of water, He wants to give us the ocean depths. God's provision always exceeds the capacity of our faith!

The third lesson we can learn from Israel's experience is *drinking from the river does not guarantee future success*. The Israelites failed despite their supernatural surroundings. They drank in God's provision yet died in sin. Although they were recipients of all the blessings of God, they never advanced beyond the wilderness. They never moved from their place of *privilege* as the *people* of God *among* the nations to their place of *purpose* as the *priests* of God *to* the nations.

Today the Church in the midst of renewal faces the same danger. We bask in the river, soaking in the blessings and refreshing of God, savoring our sense of deeper fellowship with Him. If we are not careful, we will get too content in this state and never move ahead into the full purpose of God for the Church. Paul Cain has a saying that "very few people survive the anointing." Many drink in the blessings but few take up the burdens. Many *seek* out the *presence of* God, but few *search* out their *purpose in* God!

FIRED UP OR BURNING OUT?

We live in a day when pastors and other ministers are burning out at a faster rate than ever before. According to a recent report in *Family News From Dr. James Dobson,*

> "Thousands of spiritual leaders are barely hanging on from day to day. Our surveys indicated that 80 percent of pastors and 84 percent of their spouses are discouraged or are dealing with depression. More than 40 percent of pastors and 47 percent of their spouses report that they are suffering from burnout, frantic schedules and unrealistic expectations. We estimate that approximately 1,500 pastors leave their assignments each month, due to moral failure, spiritual burnout or contention within their local congregations."[1]

H.B. London, Jr., in an article entitled "Pastoral Pressure Takes Its Toll," quotes Southern California psychiatrist Richard Blackmon: "Pastors are the single most occupationally frustrated group in America." Blackmon reported further that 30 to 40 percent of religious leaders eventually drop out of the ministry while as many as 75 percent experience periods of stress so great that they consider quitting. The incidence of mental breakdown is so high that insurance companies charge ministers four percent extra for coverage compared to employees of other businesses. The article states further that "the demand to be on call for a congregation 24 hours a day as personal confidant, marriage counselor, and crisis intervention puts church leaders in a constant whirlwind of stressful events."[2] I heard of one 55-year-old pastor who ran away from his congregation and spent three nights wandering the snow-covered mountains of San Diego. When the authorities found him, he told them he was was overwhelmed by life and just needed to get away.

A 1991 survey of pastors conducted by the Fuller Institute of Church Growth revealed these disturbing facts:

- 90% of pastors work more than 46 hours per week.
- 80% believe that pastoral ministry is affecting their families negatively.
- 33% say that being in ministry is clearly a hazard to their families.

- 75% have reported a significant crisis due to stress at least once in their ministry.
- 50% felt unable to meet the needs of the job.
- 90% felt that they were not adequately trained to cope with the ministry demands placed upon them.
- 40% reported a serious conflict with a parishioner at least once a month.
- 70% of pastors do not have someone they would consider a close friend.
- 37% have been involved in inappropriate sexual behavior with someone in the church.
- 70% have a lower self-image after they've pastored than before they started.[3]

If this is the state of so many of the trained, professional pastors and other ministers in our churches, then what is the condition of those they serve? I believe that a survey of the non-ministerial people in our churches would reveal similar levels of discouragement, stress, and burnout.

CHARISMA OR CHARACTER?

I am convinced that much of believer burnout (like "shooting stars") at all levels stems from a lack of personal intimacy with God. We have become very professional. We have focused on the externals at the cost of a true inner life. *A major problem in the Church today is that we emphasize charisma more than character.* I have told the students at Brownsville Revival School of Ministry that the Word of God teaches that the gifts of the Spirit—along with blessing and even authority—can be bestowed by the laying on of hands. However, there is not a single verse, either in the Old Testament or the New Testament, that says character can be imparted through the laying on of hands. Character can be forged in our lives only on the anvil of experience and with the hammer of obedience to God and His Word.

What do I mean by saying that we emphasize charisma more than character? Often we tend to be captivated by a person with a dynamic personality, infectious smile, or enthusiastic display of empty rhetoric. He may speak well and have a compelling message. She might have a beautiful and powerful singing voice. Perhaps he is a celebrity of some kind, a former athlete or secular recording star who has come to Christ. Natural talents or renown are fine as far as they go, but they tell us nothing about that person's character. We live in a society today that, in general, gives little thought to questions of character.

Sometimes we in the Church make the same mistake. In past years there were several highly publicized instances of major Christian leaders with powerful ministries and large followings falling into disfavor because of moral or ethical failures. We hear of popular Christian singers and recording artists having affairs or getting divorces. It is all a question of character. We have become so performance-oriented and so celebrity-focused that we are willing to excuse a leader's character flaws as long as he or she can "put on a good show," create a lot of excitement, draw a big crowd, or make us feel good.

We are in danger of forgetting how seriously God takes the matter of character in His people. God is very jealous for His name, His glory, and His honor. "I am the Lord, that is My name; I will not give My glory to another, nor My praise to graven images" (Is. 42:8). God is holy and expects all who claim His name to be holy. "Thus you are to be holy to Me, for I the Lord am holy; and I have set you apart from the peoples to be Mine" (Lev. 20:26). "But like the Holy One who called you, be holy yourselves also in all your behavior; because it is written, 'You shall be holy, for I am holy' " (1 Pet. 1:15-16).

Consider Moses. Here was this great man of God, this mighty leader of a nation, a man with whom the Scripture says God spoke "face to face, just as a man speaks to his friend" (Ex. 33:11a). Yet God denied Moses the opportunity to enter the Promised Land with the people and took his life on Mount Pisgah. Why? Because Moses misrepresented God before the people (see Num. 20:1-13). "But the Lord said to Moses and Aaron, 'Because you have not believed Me, to treat Me as holy in the sight of the sons of Israel, therefore you shall not bring this assembly into the land which I have given them' " (Num. 20:12). The Scriptures make it clear that God took Moses' life; Moses did not die of old age or natural causes. "So Moses the servant of the Lord died there in the land of Moab, according to the word of the Lord....Although Moses was one hundred and twenty years old when he died, his eye was not dim, nor his vigor abated" (Deut. 34:5,7). In other words, physically and mentally, Moses was still going strong when he died.

Moses died because he failed to display God's holiness before the people at the waters of Meribah. True holiness requires character, and holiness can be achieved only through an intimate relationship with the holy God. Knowing God intimately is the only way that we can learn to be holy as He is. Our problem is that we are too easily satisfied with the "feel good" atmosphere of exciting meetings and powerful manifestations of the Spirit. We are content to pursue an "experience" rather than the God behind the experience. We crave the "anointing" while forgetting that God's anointing does not automatically result in holiness or true spirituality. We traded "closet consciousness" for "platform consciousness"; we seek exposure before people rather than hiddenness before God. We left the prayer closet and can't find our way back. We settled for the "charisma" of the moment over the "character" of a disciplined walk in the Spirit. However, charisma will take us only so far. It is character that will carry us all the way to the finish line.

THE PROBLEM OF INTIMACY

Lack of intimacy with God, whether on the part of pastors, other "professional" ministers, deacons, other church leaders, or the believer in the pew, opens the door to all sorts of worldliness, corruption, doctrinal error, fleshly lusts, and spiritual ignorance. If we establish our lives on a religious "experience" or ritual alone rather than on a growing relationship with a living Lord, we set ourselves up to be short-lived shooting stars with no lasting influence. A good biblical example of this is the sons of Eli.

> *Now the sons of Eli were worthless men; they did not know the Lord and the custom of the priests with the people. When any man was offering a sacrifice, the priest's servant would come while the meat was boiling, with a three-pronged fork in his hand. Then he would thrust it into the pan, or kettle, or caldron, or pot; all that the fork brought up the priest would take for himself. Thus they did in Shiloh to all the Israelites who came there. Also, before they burned the fat, the priest's servant would come and say to the man who was sacrificing, "Give the priest meat for roasting, as he will not take boiled meat from you, only raw." And if the man said to him, "They must surely burn the fat first, and then take as much as you desire," then he would say, "No, but you shall give it to me now; and if not, I will take it by force." Thus the sin of the young men was very great before the Lord, for the men despised the offering of the Lord. ...Now Eli was very old; and he heard all that his sons were doing to all Israel, and how they lay with the women who served at the doorway of the tent of meeting* (1 Samuel 2:12-17,22).

Eli was the priest at Shiloh during the final years of the period when Israel had judges, shortly before Saul was anointed as the first king. Eli's sons, Hophni and Phinehas, had been anointed priests like their father, but they were "worthless men" who "did not know the Lord." This is significant. How can you truly and faithfully represent a God you don't even know? It's impossible. Their not knowing God was the fundamental condition that led to the overall sorry situation that developed. Their spiritual foundation was wrong.

How grateful I am to have had the privilege of working for 15 years in New Zealand with a senior man of God who insisted that, before I ever arrived at the church office to commence my daily responsibilities, I spend a minimum of one hour on my face before God. Thank God for a man who knew the importance of putting my spiritual relationship before the responsibilities of the church. I will be eternally grateful for his wisdom and insights, which have now become an established part of my daily routine.

Not only did Hophni and Phinehas not know the Lord, they also did not know the "custom of the priests with the people" (nor did they care). Because their spiritual foundation was wrong, their motivation for ministry was wrong. They were concerned about their own personal gain and benefit, not for the spiritual welfare of the people. They took the best of the offerings for themselves and blatantly disregarded the laws of God regarding the offering of the sacrifices.

The law said that the fat of the sacrifice belonged to the Lord, yet Eli's sons insisted on taking it for themselves. In their selfish motivation, they overstepped their proper authority as priests; they forcefully seized anything they wanted from the offerings the people brought to the Lord. Hophni and Phinehas refused to submit themselves to God or to regard themselves as servants of the people before God. They were men who exercised no restraint or self-control, readily indulging every lust or desire of body or mind, even to the point of engaging in immoral sexual relations with the women who "served at the doorway of the tent of meeting." Consequently, they had an evil reputation among the people. As priests of God, their attitudes and behavior defiled God's name. God, ever jealous for His name and His glory, brought judgment on Hophni and Phinehas. They died in battle against the Philistines.

The sons of Eli were proud, arrogant, selfish, greedy, immoral, and evil men who took advantage of the people for their own benefit. And it all stemmed from lack of intimacy: They did not know the Lord.

Regretfully, we see this same selfish motivation throughout the Body of Christ today. God's sheep are repeatedly "fleeced" by hirelings who have little or no spiritual concern for God's people. Instead they simply use the people to further their own ministry and ends. One glaring example of this is the excessive and exorbitant "registration fees" that are being charged in order to hear the Word of God. A friend of mine who worked with one of the "big" ministries told me that the first question that followed their conferences was, "How much money did we make?" I believe that God's people are growing tired of the entrepreneurial spirit that has possessed the Body of Christ.

In *Charisma* Magazine, I found the following letter to the editor:

"My husband and I attended a large church for five years. Our pastor was arrogant, solely focused on building projects and money, and could not have cared less about people. His day was spent writing books, producing tapes for which he was paid royalties and pursuing speaking engagements. He refused to have any contact with the people in the congregation.

"The sick were not visited, the grieving were given no support, the newly saved were left undiscipled, and hundreds walked out the back door of the church unnoticed. I came to view the church as yet another moneymaking business.

"We left that church and do not care to ever again become affiliated with a church. I do not view myself as unforgiving; I am just sickened by what passes for shepherds these days."

Michigan[4]

Here we have a very clear, modern-day example of the sin of Eli's sons: a minister whose sole interest is in self-service.

KEYS TO LONGEVITY

Long-term consistency in the Christian life requires that you have God-like character. To develop God-like character, you must have a life of faith that is characterized by *holiness* and *intimacy*. One of the keys to holiness is understanding God's "culture" (ways)—learning how to establish in your life an environment or dwelling that is suitable and acceptable for Him. Part of achieving greater intimacy with God is learning what it really means to worship Him "in spirit and truth" (see Jn. 4:24). Neither can be had without the other. It is impossible to learn holiness without intimately knowing the holy God. Likewise, it is impossible to know the holy God intimately without coming to Him in holiness. They go together.

Holiness and intimacy with God—the foundation stones of God-like character—do not happen overnight. No laying on of hands will impart them, fully mature, to a believer. There are no shortcuts, no quick and easy formulas. Godlike character develops over time. It is pounded out in the crucible of everyday life. It requires commitment, patience, faith, discipline and self-control. Intimacy and holiness are God's desire for all His children. Not only are they our best protection against becoming "shooting stars," which burn out and disappear before we finish the course, but they also, as they grow to maturity in our lives, lead us into the full purposes of God

ENDNOTES

1. *Family News From Dr. James Dobson*, Colorado Springs: Focus On the Family, Issue #8, August, 1998.

2. H.B. London, Jr. "Pastoral Pressure Takes Its Toll," *The Pastor's Weekly Briefing*, Colorado Springs: Focus On the Family, Vol. 7, #7, February 12, 1999.

3. Statistics are from a survey of pastors conducted by the Fuller Institute of Church Growth, as reported by Dr. Arch Hart of Fuller Theological Seminary at the Care Givers Forum, Glen Eyrie Conference Center, Colorado Springs, Colorado, November 7-10, 1991.

4. Reprint permission granted by *Charisma*.

Chapter Two

Running the Race

IMAGINE what it must have been like to travel with one of the greatest preachers and teachers of all time—the apostle Paul. This radical apostle radiated the very presence of God everywhere he went. Signs and wonders followed his ministry. Here was a mightily anointed man moving in apostolic power. Paul was given such incredible revelations from God that a messenger of satan was dispatched just to keep him humble. What must it have been like to travel with this great servant of God, to hear him preach, pray, prophesy, and proclaim God's Word day after day! Talk about privilege.

We know from reading God's Word that Demas was a part of Paul's privileged inner circle, chosen by Paul to accompany him on his travels. I doubt that there is a seminary student anywhere who would not give up his most treasured possession to have this privilege.

Demas, however, turned his back on Paul and headed into the world he loved (see 2 Tim. 4:10). Like so many "shooting stars" since then, his ministry faded like a passing fancy. His name has reverberated down through the centuries as a warning to those who have been blessed to sit under great men of God and the moving of God's Spirit, yet who never lost their lust for the world or brought their carnal desires under the control of the Holy Spirit. Like the Israelites who departed from Egypt, Demases have a glorious start but end tragically.

Unlike Demas, Paul was not a "shooting star." He was in for the long haul. Paul was a marathon runner, not a sprinter. What set him apart? His letter to Timothy reveals some clues. He writes, "I have fought the good fight, I have finished the course, I have kept the faith; in the future there is laid up for me the crown of righteousness, which the Lord, the righteous Judge, will award to me on that day; and not only to me, but also to all who have loved His appearing" (2 Tim. 4:7-8). These are the words of a winner, someone who is confidently expecting a victory celebration. These are the words of a man focused on one thing and only one thing: reaching the prize.

WHAT RACE?

As we saw in the previous chapter, one of Paul's favorite ways to describe the Christian life was to liken it to a race. This is the image he had in mind when he said, "I have finished the course." What was this "course" that Paul had run? He described it this way to the elders of the Ephesian church: "But I do not consider my life of any account as dear to myself, in order that I may finish my course, and the ministry which I received from the Lord Jesus, to testify solemnly of the gospel of the grace of God" (Acts 20:24).

Paul was determined to complete the race. The course lay clearly before him—to faithfully proclaim the gospel—and he pressed forward toward the finish line. Paul wasn't a quitter—no "burnout" for him! Instead, he was willing to be "poured out as a drink offering" (2 Tim. 4:6) for his Lord. Paul understood that there is no prize without pain, no reward without discipline, no victory without vision. Paul was proud of his King and sought to honor Him in everything he did. He was not slipshod about his conduct. As far as Paul was concerned, honoring Christ meant giving everything he had. "For to me, to live is Christ, and to die is gain" (Phil. 1:21).

One reason for Paul's discipline and determination to finish his race was his realization of the magnitude of grace and mercy that God had extended to him. He was continually amazed at the way God had reached down into his life. Paul was grateful beyond measure to the Lord who had forgiven his sins and given him eternal life, as well as the privilege of being an apostle.

Paul recognized that he had been given a precious and sacred trust and that he was responsible to God for how he handled it. For Paul, ignoring God's call on his life was unthinkable. God Himself had chosen Paul for his ministry as an apostle (see Gal. 1:15-16). As a result, Paul was determined to be faithful to his calling and firm in his commitment.

UNDER COMPULSION TO PREACH THE GOSPEL

From the day of his conversion to Christ to the day he took his last breath, Paul's compelling passion was to preach the gospel to the lost. It consumed him so completely that he could no more have refused to preach than he could have refused to breathe. "For if I preach the gospel, I have nothing to boast of, for I am under compulsion; for woe is me if I do not preach the gospel" (1 Cor. 9:16). Paul's compulsion was similar to that of Jeremiah when that prophet said, "But if I say, 'I will not remember Him or speak anymore in His name,' then in my heart it becomes like a burning fire shut up in my bones; and I am weary of holding it in, and I cannot endure it" (Jer. 20:9).

ISRAEL'S ROLE

This compulsion of Paul's to preach the gospel and so spread life to the nations was to have been the passion of the entire nation of Israel. T. Austin Sparks explains it this way:

> "What was God's intention in this world concerning the first Israel? It was that they should mediate light and life to the nations. That was their divine calling—that the nations should receive life through their light; that they should be the channel of divine light and life to the nations of this world....[For example] If it had not been for [Joseph] that whole nation would have perished, and not only the sons and families of Jacob, but all Egypt. In a sense that world would have perished. God's strange, sovereign dealings with Joseph brought him, through death and resurrection, to the throne....Life and light came not only to all the families of Jacob, but to Egypt, the world, through Joseph. He was the inclusive representative of all his brethren. God made him like that, and he sets forth this truth that God intended all Israel of old to be a minister of life and light to the whole world. That was Israel's calling and what they were intended for in the old dispensation. They were just down here by God's appointment, right at the centre of the nations, in a position of ascendancy, in order to mediate light and life to the nations. Abraham's seed was intended to do that, but that seed failed God, and instead of fulfilling their calling, they contradicted it."[1]

This was Heaven's vision for every believer's life; the heart of God was to reach the lost. Paul knew that he was part of that vision, and he never lost sight of it.

> *For though I am free from all men, I have made myself a slave to all, that I might win the more. And to the Jews I became as a Jew, that I might win Jews; to those who are under the Law, as under the Law, though not being myself under the Law, that I might win those who are under the Law; to those who are without law, as without law, though not being without the law of God but under*

the law of Christ, that I might win those who are without law. To the weak I became weak, that I might win the weak; I have become all things to all men, that I may by all means save some. And I do all things for the sake of the gospel, that I may become a fellow partaker of it (1 Corinthians 9:19-23).

LAYING ASIDE EVERY ENCUMBRANCE

Paul was probably very near the end of his life when he wrote to Timothy, "I have fought the good fight, I have finished the course, I have kept the faith" (2 Tim. 4:7). Whenever Paul talked about the race, he talked in terms not simply of finishing but of *winning*. It was not enough to be *in* the race; Paul was determined to win—to fulfill God's purpose for him—and he wanted every other believer to do so as well.

Paul learned through experience that the Christian life was a process that required diligence, commitment, and patience. His life was fraught with the most horrendous circumstances imaginable. His race was not run on an even surface; rather it was over a constantly changing obstacle course of difficulties. Yet, he kept going. Here is how Paul describes his life when contrasting it with that of the false apostles who were misleading God's flock:

Are they servants of Christ? (I speak as if insane) I more so; in far more labors, in far more imprisonments, beaten times without number, often in danger of death. Five times I received from the Jews thirty-nine lashes. Three times I was beaten with rods, once I was stoned, three times I was shipwrecked... (2 Corinthians 11:23-25).

This should encourage us to rise up in victory over our "similar difficulties"! We *can* summon the strength necessary to turn off the television and spend an hour alone with God.

You see, winning rarely happens by accident; it requires planning and preparation. Winners win because they *plan* to win. It is the focal point for all their training and preparation. Paul wrote to Timothy, "And also if anyone competes as an athlete, he does not win the prize unless he competes according to the rules" (2 Tim. 2:5). One of the "rules" that every runner knows is to get rid of any unnecessary weight or other hindrance, to strip off and set aside anything that will slow him down. You don't see someone running the mile or the marathon or the cross-country while carrying a backpack or wearing heavy boots or long, flowing clothing that would hinder leg movement.

We too are running a race.

Therefore, since we have so great a cloud of witnesses surrounding us, let us also lay aside every encumbrance, and the sin which so easily entangles us, and let us run with endurance the race that is set before us, fixing our eyes on Jesus, the author and perfecter of faith, who for the joy set before Him endured the cross, despising the shame, and has sat down at the right hand of the throne of God (Hebrew 12:1-2).

How are you running your race? Have you stripped off every encumbrance? Are you getting "in shape" so to speak? In other words, are you exercising self-control in all things in order to be fit for running the race?

PRESSING ON TOWARD THE PRIZE

Too many believers are bound by their past. They have never broken free into the "glorious liberty" God provides to all who believe and receive. When you're bound, your feet and hands are tied and you cannot run! Unfortunately, numerous children of God live under the condemnation of the accusations of the devil.

Years ago, I heard someone define the difference between condemnation and conviction. Condemnation comes when the enemy reaches into your past and brings some "past" failure or sin into the present in order to discourage you from moving on into God's purpose in the future. Conviction, however, is when the Holy Spirit brings to your remembrance some past sin in order for you to confess it, thereby freeing you to face the future with confidence and hope.

The old hymn says, "Burdens are lifted at Calvary." It's impossible to run the race while carrying some heavy burden of condemnation. God wants you free, and He supplies the grace to get free.

John Bunyon wrote a little poem, which I have carried in my Bible for years. It reads like this:

> Run John run the law demands
> But gives me neither feet nor hands
> Far better news the gospel brings
> It bids me fly and gives me wings.

The law only points to our failures and shows us our faults. But the good news of the gospel is that God supplies us with His strength and enabling grace to do all He has called us to.

Paul knew what it would take to win the race. He told the Corinthians, "Do you not know that those who run in a race all run, but only one receives the prize? Run in such a way that you may win" (1 Cor. 9:24). No one wins a race who does not give an all-out effort in the contest. A half-hearted effort does not produce a full success. Commit yourself body, soul, and spirit to the task at hand. Don't drink of the river and then die in the wilderness. Don't quit halfway through your race. Pursue your purpose till you fulfill it! If Paul were living today he would undoubtedly say, "Go for the gold."

In 1924 Eric Liddell, a Scottish runner, won the gold medal in the 400 meter race at the Paris Olympics. The son of career missionaries to China, Liddell was a committed Christian who had also felt God's call to mission work in China. At one point during his training for the Olympics he said, "I believe God made me for a purpose, for China, but He also made me fast. And when I run, I feel His pleasure." Liddell ran (and won) many races in England and Scotland and used his fame and hero status as a platform for giving testimony to Christ and how people could win the race of life by trusting in Him. After the Olympics, Liddell served the cause of Christ in China for many years, dying in a Japanese internment camp there in 1945.

Eric Liddell knew what it meant to "run in such a way that you may win." It was the only way he knew how to run, whether he was in a physical race or a spiritual race. He kept his focus on the prize, which was much more than a gold medal. For Eric Liddell, the ultimate prize was to hear the Lord whom he sought to serve and honor, say, "Well done, thou good and faithful servant…enter thou into the joy of thy lord" (Mt. 25:21 KJV).

We press toward a prize that is greater than a physical trophy for winning a race. "And everyone who competes in the games exercises self-control in all things. They then do it to receive a perishable wreath, but we an imperishable" (1 Cor. 9:25). Winners of the athletic contests in Paul's day received as prizes "simple wreaths of olive, wild celery, laurel, and pine." Those prizes would wither and die in only a matter of days. Paul looked for a prize that would not die, an imperishable wreath, "the crown of righteousness, which the Lord, the righteous Judge, will award to me on that day; and not only to me, but also to all who have loved His appearing." (2 Tim. 4:8).

So what are you striving for? It's not enough simply to be in the race; you must be determined to win. It doesn't matter whether you are old or young, male or female, or a Christian for two days or for 50 years; Paul says that you and I and everyone else are in the race. A physical race has only one winner, but wouldn't it be nice if everybody who ran got a prize, no matter where they placed? The wonderful thing about the Christian race is that, unlike the natural race, everyone can win. The Lord wants us all to win; He has planned for us to be winners. So focus on the prize and pursue it diligently, taking to heart Paul's words, "one thing I do: forgetting what lies behind and reaching forward to what lies ahead, I press on toward the goal for the prize of the upward call of God in Christ Jesus" (Phil. 3:13b-14).

KEEPING AN EYE ON THE GOAL

One of the biggest problems in the Christian Church today is that so many believers are aimless. In other words, they have trusted in Christ for salvation, but they have never surrendered their lives to His control and guidance. It is as if they have said, "Okay, I'm saved. Now what?" They have no idea, no clue, about what Jesus expects of them with regard to their lifestyle or even that they have a responsibility to live under His Lordship. In his devotional book *Awake My Heart*, J. Sidlow Baxter remarks:

"It is possible to have a saved soul and a lost life! That is because there are those who believe on Christ for the salvation of the soul from damnation in eternity, yet never hand over their life to Him, thus failing to render Spirit-filled service here, and to receive reward hereafter."[2]

In other words, you can get to Heaven by the grace of God and the blood of the Lamb, yet stand there with absolutely nothing to present to the Lord. In that case, your whole life will have been wasted, consumed by your own will, flesh, and desires. We need to recognize that, according to God's Word, He has saved us and called us. Most Christians readily acknowledge that they have been saved, but all too few fail to understand that they are called. I'm convinced that when the writer to the Hebrews speaks about pressing on to maturity, he has more in mind than repentance from "sin" when he refers to not laying again a foundation of repentance from dead works. I believe he is exhorting the believers to lay aside unprofitable activities, ways of life that have no eternal value to them. Too many Christians have given up their "sins" but continue to be involved in things that do not advance the Kingdom of God or His purpose. Scripture teaches us that one day all our "works" will be tested with fire. Any whose works pass through the fire will receive a reward, but for those whose work is burned up, "he shall suffer loss; but he himself shall be saved, yet so as through fire" (1 Cor. 3:15b). Many believers are walking aimlessly through life, building "works" of flesh that will not survive the fire of testing.

Paul was not aimless; he had a vision and a direction to his life. He knew what he wanted, where he was going, and how to get there. Keeping his eyes squarely on the goal, Paul disciplined himself for the race. He said, "I buffet my body and make it my slave" (1 Cor. 9:27a). "Buffet" is a translation of the Greek word *hupopiazo*, which literally means "to hit under the eye." In a figurative sense it refers to subduing one's passions.[3] In either sense self-control is involved. Many Christians face defeat and failure because they lack self-control; they are slaves to their passions and desires.

On the other hand, like any well-trained athlete, Paul was disciplined in every area of his life, having brought every fleshly passion and every human desire under strict subjection and control.

When I was in high school I ran the mile and some cross-country and was on the wrestling team for a while. One thing my wrestling coach stressed to all of us was the need to keep our bodies strictly under weight limits. Even a few extra pounds could put us in a higher weight category and at a disadvantage against other wrestlers who might be bigger and stronger. I remember him telling us, "If I ever catch you at McDonald's, you're done for." We were given special passes for the cafeteria that authorized us to eat the athletic meal prepared especially for the students involved in various sports. The goal was to make sure that we were in top physical condition and had our appetites under control.

The ancient Olympics that were held in Paul's day consisted primarily of footracing events. The Corinthian games, with which Paul may have had particular reason to be familiar, were second only to the Olympics. One common strategy in these events was to try to distract competing runners by rolling balls of solid gold across their paths. That would be the equivalent today of dangling several thousand dollars in front of an athlete's face. If the ploy worked, the runner would slow down to pick up the ball, losing a few precious seconds of time. Not only that, but the added weight of the heavy gold also would slow him down, resulting in his losing the race. Athletes had to learn to maintain strict self-control even in the midst of tempting distractions.

CROSSING THE FINISH LINE

Not only was Paul consumed with running a good race preaching the gospel and reaching the lost, he also was consumed with crossing the finish line in victory. He exercised self-control in all things in order to ensure that he did not fall or falter along the way or fail to complete the commission that the Lord had given him. Paul did not want to disappoint or let down the one who had been so gracious and merciful to him. He says, "I buffet my body and make it my slave, lest possibly, after I have preached to others, I myself should be disqualified" (1 Cor. 9:27). The Greek word for "disqualified" is *adokimos*, which "signifies not standing the test, rejected...i.e., disapproved, and so rejected from present testimony, with loss of future reward."[4] The word was primarily applied to the testing of metals,[5] as in assaying gold or silver to determine their level of purity, or in proving the strength, quality, or temper of the iron used for sword blades or spear heads. Metals that did not pass the test were rejected as unworthy and useless.

By using the word *adokimos* Paul is saying that all who are in the race face testing. We face the tests of integrity; of purity; of financial accountability; of carnality, ambition, and pride; and of authority. (Or, in other words, are we controllers or do we have a servant's heart?) Paul doesn't want to come to the end of the race only to find himself disqualified or rejected or to discover that he is no longer usable. (Remember that we are talking about *rewards* here, about winning the *prize*.)

When Paul stood before the Roman governor Felix defending himself against false charges brought against him by Jewish religious leaders, he said, "I also do my best to maintain always a blameless conscience both before God and before men" (Acts 24:16). The phrase "do my best" also could be translated as "exercise" or "strive." Paul's goal was to live every day with a clean conscience before both God and men, faithfully obeying the Lord and faithfully discharging his responsibility before men to proclaim Christ to them in word and action. He aspired to nothing less than to be pure in the sight of both God and man every day. That's quite a goal!

Paul was faithful to his mission, the special course that God had laid out for him. The course that God has laid out for each of us may not be the same course as Paul's, but we are all in the same race. Each of us has a particular course to run that God has set for us. According to J. Sidlow Baxter,

> "...the Christian life is to be viewed as a race, by every Christian believer....[The Lord] has a special, individualistic track of service marked out for each of us, whoever and whatever we may be. As in a physical race there is a track, a goal, and a prize, so in this spiritual race there is a track, a goal, and a prize. As in a physical race there are spectators, so in this spiritual race there are spectators—some encouraging, some discouraging. As in a physical race the runners discard all hindering weights and hampering indulgences, so in this spiritual race we must 'lay aside every weight and the sin which doth so easily beset us' (Heb. 12:1). As in a physical race the runners concentrate with keen determination to press on, so in this spiritual race *we* must concentrate with keen determination to press on. As in a physical race the runners keep their eye on the winning post and the prize, so must *we* keep our eyes on the goal and the heavenly prize."[6]

Paul's words to Timothy should be an inspiration, an encouragement, and a challenge to us. "I have fought the good fight, I have finished the course, I have kept the faith; in the future there is laid up for me the crown of righteousness, which the Lord, the righteous Judge, will award to me on that day; and not only to me, but also to all who have loved His appearing"

(2 Tim. 4:7-8). Let us be committed to run a good race with discipline and self-control, not dropping out along the way. Let us not drink from the river, only to die in the wilderness. Rather, let us press forward to the goal of fulfilling God's purpose for our lives!

ENDNOTES

1. T. Austin Sparks, *The On-High Calling*, Vol. 1 (London: Witness and Testimony Literature Trust, 1963), 75-76.

2. J. Sidlow Baxter, *Awake My Heart* (Grand Rapids, Michigan: Zondervan Publishing House, n.d.), 260.

3. James Strong, *Strong's Exhaustive Concordance of the Bible* (Peabody, Massachusetts: Hendrickson Publishers, n.d.), **hupopiazo**, (#G5299).

4. W.E. Vine, Merrill F. Unger, and William White, Jr., *Vine's Complete Expository Dictionary of Old and New Testament Words* (Nashville, Tennessee: Thomas Nelson Publishers, 1985), **cast**, New Testament section, 92.

5. Vine, Unger, and White, *Vine's Complete Expository Dictionary*, **reject**, New Testament section, 527.

6. Baxter, *Awake My Heart*, 326.

Chapter Three

They Drank From the River...

"AND we rejoice, for the river is here." So go the words of a popular song. Yes, indeed, the river is here. We are beginning to see "rivers in the wilderness." Our dry, barren lives are being touched by the hand of God as we experience a new season of refreshing from the presence of the Lord. As I crisscross the nation these days, I'm seeing a new hunger for the Spirit of God. Multitudes are being refreshed, revived, and restored. I have listened personally to numerous testimonies of how the "river" has changed and transformed their lives. As Ezekiel 47:9c states, "So everything will live where the river goes." "Everything" includes doctors, lawyers, businessmen, drug addicts, prostitutes, teenagers, and even young children.

There is nothing as exciting as listening to the testimony of a radically transformed life. Thank God for the river. May its waters increase and multitudes begin to experience firsthand the refreshing that God alone can provide.

But, although I rejoice with all those who have found refreshing at the river, I'm concerned that we don't mistake the river for the finish line of the race. The river is not the final goal; rather, it is a God-given spiritual boost on the journey.

It is like the cups of water that scores of spectators hold out to hot and sweaty runners of a marathon as they pass by. Aside from the refreshment and replenishing that the water provides, the gesture itself is an expression of encouragement to the runner. It's as if those watching are saying, "We're with you. You're doing fine. Hang in there." The water refreshes the body while the encouragement refreshes the spirit.

WATER: KEY TO LIFE

Water is absolutely essential to physical life. No creature on earth, including man, can survive without it. Throughout human history the need for water greatly influenced the development of culture and the growth of civilization. The digging of a well determined where a new village would spring up; a confluence of rivers became the cradle of a great city or even a mighty empire; seaside towns developed a maritime industry.

Because of its inseparable link to physical life, it is not surprising that water is used throughout the Scriptures as a powerful metaphor for spiritual life. From the four rivers of Eden in Genesis 2, through Ezekiel 47 with its river flowing from the house of God, all the way to Revelation 22 and the river of life issuing from the throne of God and of the Lamb, water symbolizes the pouring forth of the life-giving Spirit of God upon the earth.

The Bible also clearly illumines man's tendency to concentrate on the natural water that refreshes the body while ignoring the spiritual water that gives life to the soul. Jesus' encounter with a Samaritan woman dealt with this very issue. After asking her to give Him a drink and listening to her surprised question as to why a Jewish man would ask a Samaritan woman for water, Jesus said to her, "If you knew the gift of God, and who it is who says to you, 'Give Me a drink,' you would have asked Him, and He would have given you living water" (Jn. 4:10). The woman did not understand, though, and asked Jesus what He would use to draw this water. She was still thinking about water that would quench her thirst for a day while Jesus wanted to give her water that would satisfy her spirit for an eternity. Jesus replied, "Everyone who drinks of this water shall thirst again; but whoever drinks of the water that I shall give him shall never thirst; but the water that I shall give him shall become in him a well of water springing up to eternal life" (Jn. 4:13b-14).

On another occasion sometime later Jesus was in Jerusalem during the Feast of Tabernacles. On the last day of the weeklong festival, after the priests had carried the ritual libation of water from the pool of Siloam to the temple, Jesus stood and declared in a loud voice, "If any man is thirsty, let him come to Me and drink. He who believes in Me, as the Scripture said, 'From his innermost being shall flow rivers of living water' " (Jn. 7:37b-38). John says in the next verse that by this Jesus "spoke of the Spirit, whom those who believed in Him were to receive; for the Spirit was not yet given, because Jesus was not yet glorified" (Jn. 7:39).

In his Epistles, Paul demonstrated this dual significance of references to water in the Scriptures. For example, in writing to the Corinthians, Paul states plainly that the water that nourished the Israelites in the wilderness had a spiritual as well as a physical aspect.

> *For I do not want you to be unaware, brethren, that our fathers were all under the cloud, and all passed through the sea; and all were baptized into Moses in the cloud and in the sea; and all ate the same spiritual food; and all drank the same spiritual drink, for they were drinking from a spiritual rock which followed them; and the rock was Christ* (1 Corinthians 10:1-4).

It is significant also that he links this discussion in the same context as the race.

CHILDREN OF PRIVILEGE

In the closing verses of chapter 9 Paul makes the point that the life of faith is like a race, one in which every child of God takes part. Paul was in the race; so were the Corinthians. The implication is that we also run in the same race. Now in chapter 10 Paul brings Israel into the picture. Their race began in Egypt; it is where God fired the starting pistol, so to speak. The Passover lamb was killed, its blood was smeared on the doorposts, the death angel passed over, and several million Israelites with all their livestock marched out of Egypt under the mighty hand of God, following Moses, their leader.

Israel's race began with much momentum and great promise. It was a dynamic start. When the Israelites left Egypt they took with them the "plunder" of the Egyptians (see Ex. 12:35-36). God led them through the Red Sea and into the wilderness of Sinai where He provided them the "spiritual food" of manna and the "spiritual drink" of water from the rock. The cloud of God's presence guided them. It sheltered them from heat by day and His fire warmed them and lit their way by night. God's care and provision for them was complete and total. The Israelites truly were children of privilege.

Unfortunately, they did not see themselves that way. The Israelites repeatedly complained of their situation and the conditions of the wilderness. They longed to return to Egypt and the "pots of meat, when we ate bread to the full" (Ex. 16:3). They began the race but their hearts were not in it. Because of this, "God was not well-pleased" with most of them and "they were laid low in the wilderness" (1 Cor. 10:5). Out of the one million or more Israelites above the age of 20 who started out, only two finished and entered into God's purpose. Joshua and Caleb alone of all that first generation made it into the land that God had promised. That's pretty bad odds. Then Paul says, "Now these things happened as examples for us, that we should not crave evil things, as they also craved" (1 Cor. 10:6). A few verses later he warns, "Therefore let him who thinks he stands take heed lest he fall" (1 Cor. 10:12). Why did Paul feel it necessary to issue such a warning?

Remember that Paul was absolutely committed to finishing the race, and he wanted to make sure the Corinthian believers would finish also. Paul used Israel's wilderness experience as an object lesson to emphasize the fact that how we begin is not as important as how we finish. Israel began with great privilege. God provided for their every need. He fed them, furnished water for them, kept their clothes from wearing out, protected them, led them, and best of all, gave them His divine presence in their midst. Despite these advantages, the children of privilege failed spiritually. Paul wanted to make sure that the Corinthians—and us—didn't fail in the same way.

I thank my God always concerning you, for the grace of God which was given you in Christ Jesus, that in everything you were enriched in Him, in all speech and all knowledge, even as the testimony concerning Christ was confirmed in you, so that you are not lacking in any gift, awaiting eagerly the revelation of our Lord Jesus Christ, who shall also confirm you to the end, blameless in the day of our Lord Jesus Christ (1 Corinthians 1:4-8).

The Corinthians were "enriched" in everything in Christ and were "not lacking in any gift." Every spiritual gift was abundantly evident at Corinth, and they were prospering both spiritually and materially. God had blessed them greatly, yet they were in danger of going back to their old lifestyle of sin. Many of the Corinthian Christians had come out of a pagan background characterized by idol worship, which included eating food that had been sacrificed to idols and engaging in ritualistic sex with temple prostitutes. These believers faced the very real threat of being sucked back into the immorality and idolatry they had left upon becoming Christians.

Like the church at Corinth, we have been blessed incredibly with privilege. Paul's lesson here for the Corinthians was to help them avoid the problems Israel fell into. We too need to learn how to avoid them. Why, after having begun so well in the faith, did the Israelites' journey end so tragically? They had everything going for them, yet they turned back in their hearts and all but two of them fell in the wilderness. In his lesson Paul first listed the privileges the Israelites enjoyed, then described how they fell.

UNDER THE CLOUD

First of all, Paul says that "our fathers were all under the cloud" (1 Cor. 10:1). What was the cloud? Exodus 13:21 says, "And the Lord was going before them in a pillar of cloud by day to lead them on the way, and in a pillar of fire by night to give them light, that they might travel by day and by night." The cloud was a sign of God's continuous presence with them. He went before them in a pillar of cloud by day and in a pillar of fire by night. The cloud or the fire never departed from them. Any moment of the day or night any Israelite could look at the cloud or the fire and see the visible evidence of God's presence in the camp.

The cloud not only signified God's presence, but it also gave evidence of His protection. Shortly after leaving Egypt, the Israelites were pursued by the Pharaoh's army. Caught with their backs to the sea, the Israelites appeared to be an easy target. However, when the Israelites moved forward *through* the sea, the pillar of cloud moved from in front of the people to their rear, hovering between them and the pursuing Egyptians (see Ex. 14:19-20). God placed Himself as a shield of protection between His people and their enemies.

The cloud also protected God's people from the harshness of their environment. The Sinai wilderness posed at least four significant potential dangers to the Israelites: scarcity of food, lack of water, intense heat by day, and intense cold at night. The biblical record makes it clear that God provided abundantly for each of these needs. Paul says that Israel was "under the cloud." While this means that the people were under God's direction and leadership, it may also mean that the cloud was not always a column that went straight up into the air but was at times more mushroom-shaped, spreading over the people like an umbrella. In this way it would have sheltered them from the burning sun and the oppressive heat of the day. (Numbers 14:14 suggests this.) In contrast, the pillar of fire at night would have provided, in addition to light, warmth against the cold night air. This may be part of the thought behind the Scripture that says, "The sun will not smite you by day, nor the moon by night" (Ps. 121:6).

When the cloud stood between Israel and Egypt, there was light on Israel's side while the Egyptians were in darkness. More than just a physical reality, this represented a significant spiritual truth: Those who know the Lord live in the light; those who do not know God are in the darkness (see Eph. 5:8). The Israelites had the remarkable privilege of living "under the cloud" of God's supernatural protection and in the light of His divine presence as His special possession. God had called them and delivered them, and He wanted to mature them and prepare them to fulfill His purpose of being a light to the nations.

Paul himself knew what it was like to come under the cloud of God's presence for His purpose. As a young Jewish zealot on his way to Damascus to persecute the Church, the cloud of God's presence overshadowed him. Paul immediately bowed in surrender. God's presence brought with it a purpose and responsibility. God spoke to him later, "For this purpose I have appeared to you to appoint you a minister and a witness..." (Acts 26:16).

Likewise, when God first appeared to Moses at the burning bush, it wasn't simply a case of Moses' having some great experience, but rather of God's charging him with a divine commission. This was true for Abraham as well as for the 120 in the upper room. Cloven tongues of fire suddenly appeared...not simply so they could bask in the experience, but that they might be filled with the spirit of power and thereby testify throughout the world to the glory of God. In the same way, this also holds true for you. God has called you into His light for His purpose.

THROUGH THE SEA

Next, Paul says that all Israel "passed through the sea" (1 Cor. 10:1). The sea was the place where God miraculously delivered the Israelites from the pursuing Egyptian army. Passing through the sea can be compared to baptism. The Israelites passed through the waters, leaving behind their old life with all its bondage, servitude, taskmasters, hardship, and sorrow. They ascended the bank on the other side raised, as it were, into newness of life. Standing there beside the sea, they saw the negative things that had controlled their lives for generations lifted forever and completely cut off. The power of sin was broken over their lives. Ahead of them lay peace, prosperity, purpose, and fulfillment. At least, that was God's plan.

We as believers have a similar experience. Before Christ, we are in darkness and in bondage to sin, lost, without God and without hope in the world. Sin was our absolute master, but Christ delivered us from it all!

Christ has set us free—free to live in righteousness and holiness before God; free to fulfill God's purpose for our lives; free to walk in intimate fellowship with Him. Since water in Scripture often symbolizes the Spirit of God, the physical sea of the Israelites has a spiritual parallel for us: "For by one Spirit we were all baptized into one body, whether Jews or Greeks, whether slaves or free, and we were all made to drink of one Spirit" (1 Cor. 12:13).

BAPTIZED INTO MOSES

Another indication of the Israelites' great privilege is that they "all were baptized into Moses in the cloud and in the sea" (1 Cor. 10:2). One of the blessings that God bestows on an obedient people is to give them good, sound leaders. The opposite is also true. When people turn away from God, one of the ways He brings judgment is to remove wise leaders and raise up foolish ones in their place. The prophet Isaiah wrote,

> *Then the Lord said, "Because this people draw near with their words and honor Me with their lip service, but they remove their hearts far from Me, and their reverence for Me consists of tradition learned by rote, therefore behold, I will once again deal marvelously with this people, wondrously marvelous; and the wisdom of their wise men shall perish, and the discernment of their discerning men shall be concealed"* (Isaiah 29:13-14).

When Israel turned its back on God and refused His kingship over their lives, God responded to their request for a king (see 1 Sam. 8:5). He gave them Saul. King David graphically describes Saul's life when David sought to bring back the ark. "Let us bring back the ark of our God to us, for we did not seek it in the days of Saul" (1 Chron. 13:3). Israel was first governed by a king who never sought God's counsel or face! Unfortunately, many leaders today fall into the same category, and God's people suffer the consequences.

Without a doubt, Moses ranks as one of the greatest leaders in history. The phrase "baptized into Moses" is almost unanimously understood by biblical scholars to mean that the Israelites were all immersed under the leadership of Moses. They acknowledged Moses as their leader. In the mind of a devout Jew, there could be no greater leader. He represented the ultimate Jew, so to speak. Moses was faithful and devoted to God, taught the people the ways of God, and led them to live according to the laws of God. What a privilege they had to be under the leadership of such a great man of God!

Likewise, the Body of Christ today has benefited from the teaching and example of a number of spiritual and godly leaders, past and present. The Church of today has a great history of God's moving in her midst, and we need to remember and appreciate the privileges of our great spiritual heritage.

FOOD FROM HEAVEN

First Corinthians 10:3 says, "and all ate the same spiritual food." The pillar of cloud and of fire afforded the Israelites shelter from the daytime heat and warmth from the nighttime chill. However, the third potential danger was scarcity of food. God met this need by providing manna that appeared day after day (except on the Sabbath), which the people gathered and ate for nourishment. This is the "spiritual food" Paul was referring to. The daily provision of manna was a visible lesson from God for His people. He wanted them to learn to rely and depend completely upon Him for everything. That is the essence of spiritual maturity. The more mature we become spiritually, the more we realize how dependent we are on God. Moses reminded the people that God "humbled you and let you be hungry, and fed you with manna which you did not know, nor did your fathers know, that He might make you understand that man does not live by bread alone, but man lives by everything that proceeds out of the mouth of the Lord" (Deut. 8:3).

The manna was a completely supernatural provision. The Israelites did not have to till the soil, plant seed, or wait until harvest. All they had to do was go out each morning (except on the Sabbath) and gather it from the ground. It was always there, rain or shine. God demonstrated His faithfulness and His ability to provide. He showed Himself worthy of the Israelites' complete trust.

The daily provision of the manna revealed God's concern for the Israelites. He has the same concern for our well-being. God cares about not only our spiritual needs, but our physical needs as well. Paul wrote to the Philippians, "And my God shall supply all your needs according to His riches in glory in Christ Jesus" (Phil. 4:19). That has always been the experience of God's people. When we trust Him, He provides for our every need. Peter encouraged the readers of his first letter to trust God. "Humble yourselves, therefore, under the mighty hand of God, that He may exalt you at the proper time, casting all your anxiety upon Him, because He cares for you" (1 Pet. 5:6-7).

I will never forget the evening in 1973 when my wife and I with our two young children were just days away from leaving New Guinea where we had been involved in missionary work. I had arrived home to find that our oldest daughter, Lisa, had come from school complaining about feeling sick. As the evening progressed, her condition grew worse. She lay on the bed saying she was unable to get up and that her head and neck ached. Since we were due to leave in a few days, all our belongings were packed— including our medical journal. Having no other resource but God, we began to pray. As we prayed, Nancy, my wife, said the Lord gave her the word *meningitis*. We had no idea at the time how serious this was. After praying we saw no apparent change and called the doctor. He arrived sometime later in the midst of a torrential downpour and, after looking at her, suggested we go immediately to the hospital. When we arrived, it was confirmed that she had indeed come down with meningitis. We rallied people to pray, and I went home to our youngest daughter while Nancy stayed in the hospital. Later, my wife told me that the only other child in the children's ward was there because of meningitis also.

As Nancy sat throughout the night hours and into the early morning praying, God spoke to her and said, "It's over. Lisa is healed." When the doctor arrived to make his rounds, Lisa was up and asking for food. The doctor's only words were, "We must have made a mistake. There's nothing wrong with her." What a faithful God we have. Not only does He supply our spiritual needs, but also our physical needs. "My God shall supply all your needs...!"

It took a while for the Israelites to learn the lesson of trust. God gave very clear and precise instructions concerning the manna. The people were to gather each day only what they needed for that day. On the morning before the Sabbath they were to gather enough for two days so that they could rest on the Sabbath. Some of the people did not listen. They tried to hoard manna by gathering more than they needed for a day. They quickly discovered that any extra manna spoiled overnight, breeding worms and developing a bad smell. The assault on their nostrils helped nail home the understanding that they needed to listen to God. Others who gathered only one day's worth on Friday morning went out to gather on Saturday morning (the Sabbath) and found no manna. Their empty stomachs that day helped them learn that God meant what He said.

I used to work with Youth With a Mission. They have a saying of, "Where God guides He provides," or "Where God leads He feeds." These words are more than just slogans with them; that trust is at the very center of everything they do. That's also the very lesson God wanted the Israelites to learn. He wanted them to trust that He would fulfill what He'd promised He would do. God wanted them to believe that His Word is reliable. He wanted them to learn how to walk and stay in the center of His will.

Eventually the Israelites learned the lesson, or at least partly. They discovered that it was easier and better to stay near the cloud and the fire—to keep close to the center of God's will—because God would take care of them. God had a way of teaching the people to stay inside His will. The manna fell only in and around the camp. Those who wanted the manna had to stay within the camp; they had to remain within the company of the congregation. Anyone who chanced to venture out on their own found themselves outside of God's divine provision—without manna.

The Israelites were children of privilege because they were the recipients of the great and abundant provision of God. The Lord has not changed. Just as He provided for the Israelites in the wilderness, so He will provide for every need of all who trust Him.

WATER FROM THE ROCK

The next privilege in Paul's list that the Israelites enjoyed is they "all drank the same spiritual drink, for they were drinking from a spiritual rock which followed them; and the rock was Christ" (1 Cor. 10:4). The incident that Paul refers to occurred when the Israelites camped at Rephidim and complained to Moses because there was no water to drink. At God's direction Moses took his staff and struck a rock, which then poured forth water for the people. Moses named the place Massah (which means "testing") and Meribah (which means "quarreling") because it was there that the Israelites tested the Lord and quarreled against Moses (see Ex. 17:1-7).

It was "spiritual drink" because God provided it supernaturally. Psalm 114:8 says of God, "Who turned the rock into a pool of water, the flint into a fountain of water." Flint is one of the hardest of all stones. When I was a boy in England I used to pick up pieces of flint from the street. At night in bed I would get under the covers and strike two pieces together and watch the sparks. The old flintlock muskets used a hard piece of flint to make a spark that would ignite the gunpowder. Although flint is a very hard stone, God broke it open in the wilderness and brought forth a river to refresh His people.

Clearly, Paul attached much more than a simple natural meaning to Israel's experience at Rephidim. For him the event had great spiritual significance. The Israelites drank "from a spiritual rock which followed them; and the rock was Christ." Paul knew that the water had a divine source and a greater purpose than simply to quench physical thirst. The river from the rock represented the very power and purpose of God being brought to bear in the lives of the people He had chosen to be a light to the nations. As the Israelites drank from the river at Rephidim, trusting themselves to God's will and care, the spiritual river which was Christ (the Anointed One) renewed, refreshed, and nourished their spirits. By learning to rely on God for their physical needs they were also learning how to be spiritual children of God.

CHILDREN OF PURPOSE

The Israelites had everything going for them. They were protected, fed, and clothed; no one could have been better equipped for running a spiritual "race" than the young nation of Israel was. They got off to a great start, blessed with every spiritual blessing in Christ.

Despite their overwhelming advantages, they fell short of the goal. Paul writes, "Nevertheless, with most of them God was not well-pleased; for they were laid low in the wilderness" (1 Cor. 10:5). What happened? How could such a promising start end in such disappointment? How did such a people of privilege lose it all? Why did such a well-equipped group of "runners" fail to finish the race?

Paul lists some of the reasons: idolatry, immorality, testing God, and grumbling against God. In verse 6 he warns that we "should not crave evil things, as they also craved." Since Israel's experience is an example for us, "written for our instruction" (1 Cor. 10:11), what does this mean?

Too often we tend to regard the Bible almost as a history book that has little practical or relevant application to our own lives. This is a mistake. The Word of God is living and carries a prophetic application for every generation. So let's look at ourselves again. God has given us tremendous privileges today. Many of us have experienced "the river" and are flowing in the blessing and refreshing of God. If that is all they remain for us—just blessing and refreshing—if we never move beyond the privilege to the purpose God has in it, then we are in the same danger that both Israel and the Corinthian church were in.

Privilege is not everything. There is more than just the "river." Privilege only goes so far. Israel's experience has several important lessons for us.

- *Privilege does not guarantee us immunity from trials and problems.* Just because the Israelites drank from the river did not mean that they didn't have challenges, problems, trials, or temptations to face. There were many. The people, however, proved unwilling to follow God through the challenges into the fullness of His purpose for them. They loved the privileges and the blessings, but they were not interested in the responsibility that went with them.

- *Privilege is not the same as character.* God's benefits reveal His nature toward us, but they don't say anything of our relationship toward Him necessarily. The privilege He gives us portrays the blessings and goodness of God; it reveals nothing about who we are inside. Privilege is a gift; character must be grown. I knew a man in Seattle who was miraculously and completely healed of a severe back problem that had all but crippled him. A few weeks after his healing he confessed to me an incestuous relationship that he had with his high-school age daughter dating back to her very young childhood. I could have thought of many people I knew who needed healing and who were walking close to God and, in my mind, more "deserving" than this man was. Yet God healed him. Privilege is a gift; it says nothing about character.

- *Privilege does not free us from personal responsibility.* I fear that many of us today who are "in the river" greatly tend to chase experiences from one meeting to another, rather than ask, "God, what is this all about? Why are You touching me; why this fresh anointing? What am I supposed to do?" We run the risk of living for the blessing and failing to get involved in the greater and deeper purpose of God behind it.

In his book *The God Chasers*, Tommy Tenney writes:

"One of our problems is that whenever we have good services or feel like revival has come, we tend to camp out at that spot and pull aside from our pursuit of God so we can dance around burning bushes. We get so caught up in what happened at the bush that we never go back to Egypt and set the people free!...We are too easily satisfied with things that are not quite what they ought to be. I'm pressing my point because the Church is in grave danger of once again stopping at the 'burning bush' in this wonderful visitation of God's presence. There is a greater purpose behind the meetings taking place around the world (and it isn't just for us to get blessed). God wants to break open the heavens over our cities so the people who are without God will know that He is Lord and that He loves them."[1]

God's purpose for us today is the same as it was in Israel's day. He wanted them to be a spiritual light that would bring the whole world to Him. They drank from the river; they enjoyed the benefits and the blessings as the privileged people of God, but they failed to move beyond their privilege to fulfill God's purpose. We must guard against the same thing happening to the Church in our day. Let's not get hung up about our privileges. The river is great, but we need to move beyond basking in God's blessings to pursuing God's purpose.

ENDNOTE

1. Tommy Tenney, *The God Chasers* (Shippensburg, Pennsylvania: Destiny Image Publishers, Inc., 1998), 54-55.

Chapter Four

...And Died in the Wilderness

E watched as the dead were raised, cripples were healed, and the blind received their sight. He listened as the world's finest teacher delivered the pure unadulterated Word of God. Day after day, he beheld the very glory of God as it was revealed through His Son, the Lord Jesus Christ. Talk about a man "under the cloud"—this man was immersed into One greater than Moses. Yet, he ended his life by hanging himself and went down in history as the one referred to by "in the night in which He was betrayed." Yes, Judas was counted among the 12, but he "died in the wilderness."

If his were the only case of its kind, it would be tragic. Unfortunately, his was just the beginning of a long and terrible list of servants who began with God's anointing, but who failed because of a lack of self-control. Judas had a problem with money. The silver meant more to him than the Savior. He traded the Master for mammon.

In the past decade alone, I can recall over and over again the lives of great televangelists, musicians, spiritual leaders, and lesser known men in ministry who have traded their "birthright" for a night of sex. Some of these men I have known and admired. Some I have worked with in ministry or been closely acquainted with. I have watched and, in the words of Job, I have seen their increase uprooted (see Job 31:9-12).

How can we avoid the same sad failure that befell these men of God and the Israelites in the wilderness of Sinai? One way is to have a better understanding of why they failed. We have already seen that their failure was not due to lack of resources or opportunity. God planned for them to succeed. God *wanted* them to succeed; He gave them everything they needed to do so. He promised to go before them, walk beside them, work through them, and overshadow them to bring them safely into the land—into the fullness of His purpose. All that remained was for the people to move forward in willing, trusting obedience. Unfortunately, that's where the problem lay.

In chapter 10 of First Corinthians Paul continues his lesson about how to run a successful race by listing the specific sins Israel indulged in before being "laid low in the wilderness."

> *Now these things happened as examples for us, that we should not crave evil things, as they also craved. And do not be idolaters as some of them were; as it is written, "The people sat down to eat and drink, and stood up to play." Nor let us act immorally, as some of them did, and twenty-three thousand fell in one day. Nor let us try the Lord, as some of them did, and were destroyed by the serpents. Nor grumble, as some of them did, and were destroyed by the destroyer. Now these things happened to them as an example, and they were written for our instruction, upon whom the ends of the ages have come. Therefore let him who thinks he stands take heed lest he fall* (1 Corinthians 10:6-12).

Greed, idolatry, immorality, rebellion, grumbling—these were the keys to Israel's undoing. Each reflects a fundamental flaw in spiritual and moral character and each is symptomatic of a lack of basic self-control. They were problems for the Corinthian church, and they continue to threaten the health and welfare of the Church in our own day. So let's examine each of these in greater detail, focusing first on greed, rebellion, and grumbling.

KEEPING UP WITH THE JONESES

Forty pair of shoes would be extravagant by most people's standards, let alone 6,000 pairs! And yet, according to the news service, for Emelda Marcos, wife of Ferdinand Marcos of the Philippines, they were just part of her elaborate and lavish style of living. Never satisfied, she kept acquiring more and more. While this is a rare case for shoes, nonetheless, we in society today have become obsessed with "things." John warns us, "Do not love the world, nor the *things* in the world. If anyone loves the world, the love of the Father is not in him" (1 Jn. 2:15).

How quickly we can turn a finger of accusation against Israel and yet practice the same things ourselves. Jesus warned us in the parable of the sower that the riches, worries, and cares of this life choke the seed, and it never brings fruit to maturity.

We live in a materialistic society. Our secular culture tells us that the continual acquisition of things is the path to success, contentment, and happiness. Supply and demand, consumption, and credit are major foundation stones in America's industrial base and economic philosophy. Not only are we encouraged to buy, buy, buy, but the wide availability of credit cries out to us to buy now, buy now, buy now, whether or not we have the money.

All this boils down to the basic problem of greed. What we have never seems to be enough; we always want more. We can't stand for a neighbor or an acquaintance to have something we don't have. The drive to "keep up with the Joneses" is enormous. Sometimes we feel that what we have is not as good as what we had once before, and we long for those earlier things. In either case we are not satisfied with things as they are, which leads to griping and complaining and an obsession with "getting ahead." Greed increases stress, fosters discontent, and results in unfulfilled desires. A greedy spirit is never satisfied.

LONGING FOR EGYPT

This is what plagued the Israelites in the wilderness. Paul defined their greed as to "crave evil things." They became discontented with their current situation and began to long for what they had known in Egypt.

And the rabble who were among them had greedy desires; and also the sons of Israel wept again and said, "Who will give us meat to eat? We remember the fish which we used to eat free in Egypt, the cucumbers and the melons and the leeks and the onions and the garlic, but now our appetite is gone. There is nothing at all to look at except this manna" (Numbers 11:4-6).

Look at the effect greed had on their spirit. Growing tired of manna, the Israelites longed for the variety of food they had known in Egypt. No matter that Egypt represented slavery, hardship, and darkness. No matter that manna and the camp in the wilderness represented freedom, deliverance, and an invitation to be involved in God's purposes. All they cared about was their stomachs. They were tired of the daily breakfast cereal, so to speak. Soon they began to feel that God had short-changed them. In their minds, the rather bland manna could not compare with the rich foods of Egypt. Greed had so consumed them that they preferred a life of slavery in Egypt to a life of freedom in the presence and purpose of God—if it meant they could indulge their desires.

Although angry at the people's obstinacy and greed, God answered their cry for "meat." However, it was accompanied by judgment for their sin.

The Lord said that He would send meat not for a day or two but for a month and that the people would eat it "until it comes out of your nostrils and becomes loathsome to you; because you have rejected the Lord who is among you and have wept before Him, saying, 'Why did we ever leave Egypt?' " (Num. 11:20b) That night a wind from the Lord brought quail from the sea into the camp in such great quantities that the people spent two days simply gathering them up. As the people began to eat the quail, the judgment of God fell. "While the meat was still between their teeth, before it was chewed, the anger of the Lord was kindled against the people, and the Lord struck the people with a very severe plague. So the name of that place was called Kibroth-hattaavah, because there they buried the people who had been greedy" (Num. 11:33-34).

CRAVING THE CARNAL

Paul feared that the Corinthian Christians would follow Israel's bad example and end up being "disqualified" in the race. The Corinthians certainly did not face the prospect of the same diet every day as the Israelites did, but they had their own problems with food and other appetites. Part of their pagan past had involved going to the idol temples with their friends for wild orgies of food and sex. Eating food that had been sacrificed to idols also was common. Many of the Christian believers were reverting back to some of these old habits. Unbridled greed and uncontrolled desires threatened to destroy their witness and shipwreck their faith. Many insisted that they were free in Christ to indulge their desires, regardless of the effect their behavior had on the faith of weaker believers. This was particularly true with regard to eating meat that had been sacrificed to idols.

Greed is putting natural human desires ahead of God's desires; it is pursuing physical and carnal things at the expense of spiritual things. Left unchecked, greed can grow so large in your heart that it overcomes and consumes everything else. That is why it is so dangerous. For the Israelites it was the desire for the "good life" of Egypt (even if it meant being slaves again); for the Corinthians it was the urge to gratify fleshly lusts and abuse their freedom in Christ; for us it could be any number of things. We are in the grip of greed if there is something we desire more than God, if there is some thing (or things) more important to us than knowing the Lord and seeking to walk in His will and way.

His father was rich and generous. As the years passed by, the younger son became aware that his father had set aside a good portion of money for him and his older brother. Like any kid his age, he dreamed of what he could do if he only had the "bucks"—travel, adventure, fine clothes, food, and any possession he wanted. Going to his father, he asked and was given his inheritance.

His desire was not in opposition to his father's purpose. In fact, his father was the one who planned the inheritance. It was intended to be a great source of blessing from the father. But what started out as a blessing ended with the blunder of his life. The end result was not due to the generosity of the father, but to the failure of the son.

A desire that becomes greedy may not be evil in and of itself. It may be simply something that lies outside God's will for us at a particular time: a new and better job, a promotion, a marriage partner, a new car, a new house. Within the framework of God's will and plan these are fine. However, if we pursue them stubbornly, without regard to God's desire, we cross the line into greed. A healthy desire then becomes a craving for an evil thing. The natural overtakes the spiritual. It is so easy for us to lust after the wrong things, to put the will of the flesh before the will of God, that we must be constantly on guard.

In a chapter titled "Living in Canaan" in his book, *From Shadow to Substance*, author Roy Hession defined the word lust:

"In the Bible the word *lust* does not apply only to sex. Lust is a clamant desire that wants something and wants it now and is unsubordinated to the will of God. It is a wishing, wishing, wishing for what God has not given us. The fact that we do not have that thing means that, at the moment at least, it is not His will for us. Maybe He has it for us in the future, but we are not content to wait; we wish to have it now. Israel was wishing, wishing, wishing for the melons and onions of Egypt. But God had not given them the melons and onions of Egypt: He had given them manna. And this lusting in their hearts made them lose their taste for that which God had given them—the precious, miraculous 'bread of heaven.' 'There is nothing at all beside this manna before our eyes,' they said; 'Manna for breakfast, manna for dinner, and manna for supper!'

"Who of us does not find himself wishing sometimes for what God has not given us; perhaps for a position God has not given us, or for possessions God has not given us, or for success God has not given us. For some it may be wishing, wishing for a husband God has not given, or for children God has not given, or for a better job God has not given. This wishing always makes us lose our taste for Jesus, the heavenly manna. We just cannot say truthfully that He is satisfying us when we have this lusting for something else in our hearts."[1]

That is why self-control is so important and why Paul exercised such strict discipline over his own body. Paul was a normal man with the same natural desires and urges as anyone else. However, he learned to control them, to subject them to his will so that they would not sidetrack him or trip him up in his race for the prize. We need to be just as careful as Paul or our desires will consume us and dominate our lives. When that happens, we lose our spiritual focus and become confused about what is really important.

Moreover, those who are governed by greed stand in opposition to God. Paul stated it this way to the Philippians, "For many walk, of whom I often told you, and now tell you even weeping, that they are enemies of the cross of Christ, whose end is destruction, whose god is their appetite, and whose glory is in their shame, who set their minds on earthly things" (Phil. 3:18-19). The phrases "whose god is their appetite" and "who set their minds on earthly things" aptly describe people consumed by greed. They put the physical ahead of the spiritual and the temporal ahead of the eternal. Bearing the cross of Christ is not as important to them as gratifying their selfish, fleshly desires.

We in America face this sort of thing constantly. Just go to the nearest shopping mall. We must have that new dress or that new suit, that beautiful gold ring or necklace, that stylish tie. We must buy that new car because the neighbors just bought one, or that bigger, nicer house to keep in step with our "status." All these "things" mean more to us than serving God. They get in our way, trip us up, and threaten to prevent us from finishing the race.

TRADING IN THE BIRTHRIGHT

Esau's life is a good illustration of the consequences of confusing the importance of the carnal with the spiritual. As the elder son Esau stood to inherit the bulk of his father's estate, his home, and his name, over his twin but younger brother Jacob. The Book of Genesis describes Esau as a hunter and a man of the fields, while Jacob was more of a "homebody." One day Esau came home famished after a long, tiring hunt. Jacob had prepared some stew, the very scent of which made Esau's mouth water. When Esau asked for some of the stew, Jacob agreed to give him some in return for his birthright. With apparently no thought or hesitation, Esau agreed.

Esau exchanged his birthright for a bowl of stew. Esau's birthright represented his spiritual heritage, yet he traded it away for the immediate gratification of a passing physical desire. In a moment's time, he was willing to pay any price to satisfy his desire. The elder son of a free man, Esau was in reality a slave. He was in bondage to his physical desires and passions. They completely controlled and consumed him. His body was his master.

When Esau sold his birthright, he forfeited all the spiritual blessings of God that were his by right. Afterwards, when he realized more fully what he had done, Esau tried to regain his lost position but could not. It was too late.

The writer of Hebrews described Esau as an "immoral [and] godless person...who sold his own birthright for a single meal...[who] afterwards, when he desired to inherit the blessing, he was rejected, for he found no place for repentance, though he sought for it with tears" (Heb. 12:16-17). The word *repentance* here refers to privilege rather than salvation. Esau discovered to his sorrow that once he sold his birthright, there was no going back, no way to reclaim it. He had forfeited his privilege forever, all because he was consumed by his greed. God was not going to repent, or change His mind, because He had already given His blessing to Jacob.

Greed is no less an issue today. Examine your own life—are there "things" you have put before God? Drop those golden balls that hinder your race. Determine to pursue God's will for your life!

TRYING THE LORD

In First Corinthians 10:9 Paul writes, "Nor let us try the Lord, as some of them did, and were destroyed by the serpents." Another word for "try" is *test*: "nor let us *test* the Lord." Greed is one thing that brought the Israelites low in the wilderness; rebellion against God is another. The specific incident that Paul refers to is found in chapter 21 of the Book of Numbers:

And the people spoke against God and Moses, "Why have you brought us up out of Egypt to die in the wilderness? For there is no food and no water, and we loathe this miserable food." And the Lord sent fiery serpents among the people and they bit the people, so that many people of Israel died. So the people came to Moses and said, "We have sinned, because we have spoken against the Lord and you; intercede with the Lord, that He may remove the serpents from us." And Moses interceded for the people. Then the Lord said to Moses, "Make a fiery serpent, and set it on a standard; and it shall come about, that everyone who is bitten, when he looks at it, he shall live." And Moses made a bronze serpent and set it on the standard; and it came about, that if a serpent bit any man, when he looked to the bronze serpent, he lived (Numbers 21:5-9).

At first glance it might appear that the people's problem once again was greed; after all, they are complaining about the food and water again. At the heart of their complaint, however, was a spirit of rebellion: "The people *spoke against* God and Moses." Prior to this God had delivered a powerful Canaanite enemy into Israel's hands. Fresh from this victory they traveled around the land of Edom, and verse 4 says that "the people became impatient because of the journey." Rebellion was at the root of their complaint. They didn't want to go the way that Moses and the Lord were leading them. Perhaps they thought the road was too long or that a direct route through Edom would be quicker. At any rate, they questioned God's judgment.

Essentially, rebellion is putting God on trial. "God, can You *really* do that? Did You *really* mean what You said? Are You really true to Your Word? Can You *really* be trusted? We're not sure. We don't believe You." Psalm 78:8 calls this earliest generation of the nation of Israel "a stubborn and rebellious generation, a generation that did not prepare its heart, and whose spirit was not faithful to God." A few verses later the same psalm says,

> *And in their heart they put God to the test by asking food according to their desire. Then they spoke against God; they said, "Can God prepare a table in the wilderness? Behold, He struck the rock, so that waters gushed out, and streams were overflowing; can He give bread also? Will He provide meat for His people?" Therefore the Lord heard and was full of wrath, and a fire was kindled against Jacob, and anger also mounted against Israel; because they did not believe in God, and did not trust in His salvation* (Psalm 78:18-22).

Can you hear the rebellious, questioning tone in their words? The irony is that, according to Numbers 21:4, it was the Israelites' impatience with the journey that sparked their rebellion. The length of the journey was *their* fault. God gladly would have taken them on a quicker, more direct route into His purposes, but they were not ready. Their hearts were not prepared and their spirits were not faithful to God. The Israelites spoke against God and Moses because of their own shortcomings. Israel insisted on having its own way and then blamed God for the delay in progress.

God's anger burned against the people because of their rebellion, and He sent fiery serpents among them. Many Israelites died from the serpents' bites. Yet even in this story of rebellion and judgment we find the opportunity for repentance and restoration. Once the Israelites realized the magnitude of their sin, they appealed to Moses, who interceded for them before God. Under God's direction Moses fashioned a serpent out of bronze, mounted it on a pole, and set it in the midst of the people. Any bite victims who looked upon the bronze serpent—thereby acknowledging their trust and dependence on God for their deliverance—were healed.

Rebellion is a serious matter. God doesn't take it lightly and neither should we. Because of our sinful nature, we all are just as prone to rebel against God as the Israelites were. In fact, rebellion is at the heart of sin. The sin of Adam and Eve in the Garden of Eden was rebellion against God. In essence, they wanted to be their own gods. The root of rebellion lies in every one of us, so we must constantly and carefully guard against it lest it gain a foothold in our lives and spirits. An attitude that continually calls into question God's character, grace, mercy, love, kindness, power, and compassion ultimately will upset us in our race and keep us from fulfilling God's purpose for us.

MOUTHING OFF TO GOD

"Nor grumble, as some of them did, and were destroyed by the destroyer" (1 Cor. 10:10). Simply stated, grumbling challenges God's actions or what God has allowed. In this regard the third sin of grumbling is similar in many ways to the sins of greed and rebellion. Grumbling takes many forms. It blames God for our problems and hardships, criticizes God's actions and decisions, challenges God's wisdom and authority, gives only grudging obedience, displays a negative and critical attitude, and challenges the authority of those whom God has chosen and raised up into leadership.

The specific incident Paul refers to is found in Numbers 16. A company of 250 Israelite men led by Korah, Dathan, and Abiram challenged Moses' and Aaron's authority and questioned their leadership. In reality, they were challenging God, who had called and appointed Moses and who had consecrated Aaron as the high priest. As a result, Moses summoned each of the leaders to offer incense to the Lord. Aaron would do likewise and whichever offering the Lord accepted would indicate who His chosen leaders were. At the appointed time, fire from Heaven consumed the 250 men offering incense. The earth opened up and swallowed Korah, Dathan, and Abiram, along with their entire families and all their belongings (see Num. 16:1-35).

Such an undeniable display of God's power and will should have been enough to convince the rest of the Israelites to trust God and follow Moses, but it wasn't. "But on the next day all the congregation of the sons of Israel grumbled against Moses and Aaron, saying, 'You are the ones who have caused the death of the Lord's people' " (Num. 16:41). As a result, God's wrath in the form of a plague fell upon the people.

And Moses said to Aaron, "Take your censer and put in it fire from the altar, and lay incense on it; then bring it quickly to the congregation and make atonement for them, for wrath has gone forth from the Lord, the plague has begun!" Then Aaron took it as

Moses had spoken, and ran into the midst of the assembly, for behold, the plague had begun among the people. So he put on the incense and made atonement for the people. And he took his stand between the dead and the living, so that the plague was checked. But those who died by the plague were 14,700, besides those who died on account of Korah. Then Aaron returned to Moses at the doorway of the tent of meeting, for the plague had been checked (Numbers 16:46-50).

Grumbling is often the fruit of a rebellious heart and a spirit not yielded to God. Unbelief also plays a part. If our faith is small or if we have a stubborn spirit, it is easy for us to challenge God when things are not going well. "God, why did You let this happen? God, why are You letting me go through these hard times? Why did You do this, why did You do that, why, why, why?" Sometimes such an outcry pours from the anguished heart of a faithful believer who is simply seeking to understand. We must be very careful, though, because it is easy to let such a cry of searching faith cross the line into resentful grumbling. God always honors the honest cry of faith. Grumbling, however, has no place in the life of a child of God.

KNOWING OUR HEARTS

Sometimes God allows us to go through difficult times, through hardship and trials. During these times He may seem distant, even silent. However, everything God does, everything He allows into our lives, is for our ultimate good. That's often difficult to remember when we are in the midst of a crisis. One thing that difficulties do is reveal our "heart status." They show us the condition of our faith-life. This was one reason why the Israelites faced these challenges in the wilderness; God was testing them. Moses made this clear when he spoke to a new generation of Israelites poised to enter the Promised Land after 40 years of wandering in the wilderness.

And you shall remember all the way which the Lord your God has led you in the wilderness these forty years, that He might humble you, testing you, to know what was in your heart, whether you would keep His commandments or not. And He humbled you and let you be hungry, and fed you with manna which you did not know, nor did your fathers know, that He might make you understand that man does not live by bread alone, but man lives by everything that proceeds out of the mouth of the Lord. Your clothing did not wear out on you, nor did your foot swell these forty years. Thus you are to know in your heart that the Lord your God was disciplining you just as a man disciplines his son (Deuteron-omy 8:2-5).

God led them for 40 years in the wilderness in order to humble them and teach them to depend on Him; to test their hearts and teach them to obey Him. He fed them so that they would learn that life comes from God. He disciplined them that they might grow to maturity and be prepared to enter the land and fulfill His divine purpose. All this was for their good. "In the wilderness He fed you manna which your fathers did not know, that He might humble you and that He might test you, to do good for you in the end" (Deut. 8:16).

In other words, we shouldn't question what God allows to come into our lives because whatever He permits is for the purpose of achieving our ulti-mate good. The key to avoiding the sin of grumbling is to clearly understand the nature and character of God. It is God's love and concern for us that moti-vates everything He does. Difficulties do not come our way because God is ill-tempered or mean-spirited or because He doesn't like us. Difficulties come as a normal part of life in a fallen world, and God permits them because He knows that, if we allow them to, they will help us grow to maturity.

I have always been challenged by J.B. Phillips' translation of James 1:2-4: "When all kinds of trials and temptations crowd into your lives, my brothers, don't resent them as intruders, but welcome them as friends! Realise that they have come to test your faith and to produce in you the qual-ity of endurance. But let the process go on until that endurance is fully developed, and you will find you have become men of mature character...."

God spoke to me in an unusual way one day regarding this truth. My car was desperately in need of some new tires, so I decided to stop in at the local tire store, which happened to sell Dunlop tires. Upon entering the store, I looked up and saw a large banner advertising five to six tires. The tires ranged from their standard economy tire to the most expensive premi-um grade. Under each tire was a short summary of its characteristics. The economy grade read something to the effect that the tire was good under average conditions, etc. When I read the statistics under the premium grade, I was impressed with all the tests it had endured and never failed. This tire had been tested on all the great racetracks of Europe. It had been driven in extreme conditions and at great speeds. Just reading the advertisement con-vinced me that this was the tire for me. As I stood looking at this banner, I sensed the Lord saying, "That is how I look at My people. Some are good under average conditions, but the ones I can truly depend on are those who have been tested under the greatest trials and difficulties and yet show no sign of failure or fatigue. Rather, they have come through the tests with greater faith and trust in Me." I believe Job was that sort of man. God bragged to the devil about him, "Go ahead and test him. Drive him as hard as you like and see if he will lose his trust in Me."

God tests us for the purpose of discipline, not punishment; it is for correction and instruction so that we may be built up in faith and prepared to run a successful race. Testing and discipline help us know our own hearts so that we can love and serve the Lord with pure and true motives. We should welcome God's discipline—it is a sign that we are His children. Every loving father disciplines his children, and our heavenly Father is no different. God wants to see every one of us enter fully into His purpose. He wants to be able to look at each of us and say, "Well done, thou good and faithful servant: thou hast been faithful over a few things, I will make thee ruler over many things: enter thou into the joy of thy lord" (Mt. 25:21 KJV).

Greed, rebellion, and grumbling were three serious sins that led to the downfall of the first generation of Israelites after leaving Egypt. The final straw came when the people listened to the negative report of 10 of the 12 spies who had been sent into Canaan to survey the land (see Num. 13:1–14:24). Two of the spies, Joshua and Caleb, said that the Lord would be with them in taking the land. The other ten spies said that it couldn't be done; the Canaanite inhabitants were too strong. Heeding the negative report, the people rebelled against God, grumbled against Moses, and proposed to replace him with another leader who would take them back to Egypt. (There's that greed again.)

God had had enough. Pronouncing judgment on the people, He declared that no one of that first generation would enter the land. Their continual obstinacy forfeited their chance to "finish the race" and enter into the purpose God had for them. Joshua and Caleb were the exceptions. Because they had remained faithful, they received God's reward of entering safely into the land. But even they had to endure the 40 years in the wilderness before that promise was fulfilled.

So an entire generation died in the wilderness, outside of God's will, plan, and purpose. It remained for their children, under the leadership of Joshua, to enter in and claim the land. Almost an entire generation died in the wilderness because of unbelief. They drank from the river but died in the wilderness. They died because of greed, rebellion, and grumbling. They also died because of idolatry and immorality. All these sins are serious and pose a problem for the Church, but idolatry and immorality are so rampant today that they are particularly dangerous. We'll look at them next.

The wilderness was never God's final goal for the nation of Israel. It was to be only a place of transition, a place of growth and maturity, a temporary (and brief) interlude between Egypt and the land of Canaan. Unfortunately, the wilderness became a permanent dwelling place for them. What was intended to be the beginning part of their journey became their final resting place. Let us commit ourselves to God and run a good race so that the same thing does not become true of us!

ENDNOTES

1. Roy Hession, *From Shadow to Substance* (Grand Rapids, Michigan: Zondervan Publishing House, 1977), 39-40.

Chapter Five

Sleeping With the Enemy

LOT had everything going for him—cattle, family connections, servants. We first meet him in the Scriptures with his uncle Abram. Abram had left Haran under God's direction to go to "the land which I will show you" (Gen. 12:1), where God promised he would become a great nation through whom all the nations of the earth would be blessed. Lot was part of this company of faith that was traveling under the leadership and promise of God (see Gen. 12:4).

The next time we see Lot, both he and Abram have become so prosperous with large flocks and herds that they find it necessary to separate. Abram lets Lot choose which part of the land he will settle in; whatever part Lot chooses, Abram will take the other. Lot's choice is significant and revealing.

> *And Lot lifted up his eyes and saw all the valley of the Jordan, that it was well watered everywhere—this was before the Lord destroyed Sodom and Gomorrah—like the garden of the Lord, like the land of Egypt as you go to Zoar. So Lot chose for himself all the valley of the Jordan; and Lot journeyed eastward. Thus they separated from each other. Abram settled in the land of Canaan, while Lot settled in the cities of the valley, and moved his tents as far as Sodom* (Genesis 13:10-12).

Notice that Lot moved eastward—away from Abram's company, the company of promise—as far as Sodom. Verse 12 in the King James Version says that Lot "pitched his tent toward Sodom." The very next verse tells of the great wickedness of the men of Sodom. So, in effect, Lot moved away from the company of the righteous toward the company of the wicked.

Before long, war comes to the valley of the Jordan. The invading armies capture Lot and all his possession. By this time, Lot is *living in* Sodom (see Gen. 14:12). Fortunately for Lot, his uncle Abram takes a trained host of men, defeats Lot's captors, and releases Lot.

After this, Lot drops from the story for a bit. When he reappears, he is "sitting in the gate of Sodom" (Gen. 19:1). The gate is where the city elders sit. In the gate he greets two men who are really angels sent by God to destroy Sodom and Gomorrah for their sin and wickedness. Do you see the progression here? Lot moved from the company of righteousness *toward* Sodom, then he was *in* Sodom, and finally became, apparently, an *elder* of the city. Although Scripture does not indicate that Lot ever approved of or participated in the wickedness of Sodom, his reluctance to leave at the angels' warning reveals his attraction to the city. They had to forcibly and physically take him from the city (see Gen. 19:16).

Whatever righteous influence Lot may have had earlier appears to have diminished during his association with Sodom. When Lot tries to warn his sons-in-law of the coming destruction, they think he is joking (see Gen. 19:14). Lot's wife is even more reluctant to leave than he is. Her reluctance caused her to look back, with tragic consequences (see Gen. 19:17,26). Then, Lot's two daughters get him drunk and engage in incestuous relations with him in order to become pregnant. The sons born to them, Moab and Ben-ammi, became the fathers of the Moabites and the Ammonites, two nations that later caused trouble for Israel.

No Compromise

Lot's story is a sad one indeed. Here is a man who once had flocks and herds perhaps equaling those of his uncle Abram, prosperous and full of promise, reduced to living in a cave with his daughters (see Gen. 19:30). A man who once walked with the company of faith and promise, he fathers children whose offspring become enemies of the people of God.

Such is the subtle encroachment of sin. Sometimes all it takes is one small step off the path. That step leads to another, and another, and another—until one day we wake up and realize that we are miles farther away than we ever intended to be. Very few people deliberately *set out* to ruin their lives. It happens gradually—a little indulgence here, a little compromise there. If not checked, the cumulative effect on our lives will be tragedy, disaster, or destroyed usefulness. Remember that it's possible to have a saved soul and a lost life. You can't finish the race if you step off the course.

The Church today is in danger of falling into the same pattern. We have compromised our standards and disobeyed God's Word. We have allowed the ways of the world into our homes primarily through television and music. Consequently, we have seen a generation of our youth turn away from the things of God and become engrossed with drugs, sex, pornography, and every other area of vileness. Paul the apostle admonished Timothy with these words: "Let every one that nameth the name of Christ depart from iniquity" (2 Tim. 2:19b KJV). We need to respond afresh to the voice of the Spirit in our day that continues to say, " 'Come out from their midst and be separate,' says the Lord. 'And do not touch what is unclean; and I will welcome you. And I will be a father to you, and you shall be sons and daughters to Me,' says the Lord Almighty" (2 Cor. 6:17-18).

The Israelites did not follow God's directives. Instead, read the Psalmist's description of Israel's history in Psalm 106:34-38:

> *They did not destroy the peoples as the Lord commanded them, but they mingled with the nations, and learned their practices, and served their idols, which became a snare to them. They even sacrificed their sons and their daughters to the demons, and shed innocent blood....*

What began with disobedience to God's Word ended with mothers and fathers sacrificing their own children to demon gods.

This is why God was so severe with the Israelites. Any sin had to be rooted out immediately lest it take hold and lead all the people astray. This is also why God wanted the Israelites to completely drive out and in some cases annihilate the inhabitants of their new land. God knew that the pagan practices of the land would contaminate the Israelites. Because the Israelites failed to completely obey God's command, they struggled against these nations and their false religions for years.

It is critically important that we have an attitude of *no compromise* when it comes to sin. Anything less is courting disaster. This also is precisely why Paul was so unrelenting in his discipline and self-control. He understood the dangerously subtle nature of sin and took it very seriously. We must do the same.

The tragic lesson of Israel in the wilderness is that they did not take sin seriously and therefore paid the consequences. They squandered their blessings, destroyed their usefulness, and forfeited their opportunity to move from privilege to purpose as the children of God. Amidst the greed, rebellion, and grumbling that helped bring them down were two sins that were even worse because they were at the root of the others: idolatry and immorality. These same sins pose a particularly dangerous threat today, especially in the Church, because they are so subtle and so prevalent.

No Other Gods

Idolatry is placing anything or anyone other than God highest in our affection and allegiance; it is worshiping anything or anyone other than Him. The first two of the Ten Commandments make clear how important this matter is to God.

> *You shall have no other gods before Me. You shall not make for yourself an idol, or any likeness of what is in heaven above or on the earth beneath or in the water under the earth. You shall not worship them or serve them; for I, the Lord your God, am a jealous God, visiting the iniquity of the fathers on the children, on the third and the fourth generations of those who hate Me, but showing lovingkindness to thousands, to those who love Me and keep My commandments* (Exodus 20:3-6).

God leaves no room for doubt here: His blessings await those who love and obey Him while His judgment lies ahead for those who disobey. The two commandments are related; they go together. Although all the commandments are vital, these two (along with the third commandment, which forbids taking God's name in vain) are the only ones that have specific promises of punishment attached to them—another indication of their fundamental importance.

In First Corinthians 10:7 Paul writes, "And do not be idolaters, as some of them were; as it is written, 'The people sat down to eat and drink, and stood up to play.' " In citing idolatry, Paul quotes from Exodus 32:6. The story is familiar, though sad.

Moses is on Mount Sinai; he has been gone from the people for 40 days and nights. God has just given Moses the Ten Commandments on stone tablets. However, before the stone dust from carving the Ten Commandments could even settle, the Israelites violated them.

> *Now when the people saw that Moses delayed to come down from the mountain, the people assembled about Aaron, and said to him, "Come, make us a god who will go before us; as for this Moses, the man who brought us up from the land of Egypt, we do not know what has become of him"* (Exodus 32:1).

Aaron should have known better; nonetheless, he yielded to the people's request. Taking the gold earrings that the people offered, Aaron fashioned them into a molten calf. The people then declared, "This is your god, O Israel, who brought you up from the land of Egypt" (Ex. 32:4b). Aaron then declared the next day as a feast day to the Lord.

So the next day they rose early and offered burnt offerings, and brought peace offerings; and the people sat down to eat and to drink, and rose up to play. Then the Lord spoke to Moses, "Go down at once, for your people, whom you brought up from the land of Egypt, have corrupted themselves. They have quickly turned aside from the way which I commanded them. They have made for themselves a molten calf, and have worshiped it, and have sacrificed to it, and said, 'This is your god, O Israel, who brought you up from the land of Egypt!' " (Exodus 32:6-8)

Only the intercession of Moses prevented the immediate judgment of God from falling on the Israelites. As it was, loyal Levites went through the camp at Moses' command, killing those who had worshiped the golden calf. Three thousand people died that day, but the camp was cleansed. The Israelites learned the hard way that when God said, "You shall have no other gods before Me," He meant it.

MAN THE IMAGE-MAKER

The incident with the golden calf revealed a persistent tendency toward sin in the Israelites. For centuries the Israelites dealt with the chronic and debilitating problem of idolatry. Repeated offenses resulted in repeated judgments. Finally, the only thing that could cure Israel of their pursuit of foreign gods and the making and worshiping of graven images happened: They spent 70 years in captivity and exile in Babylon.

Fallen man has a "natural" proclivity to fashion and worship idols. Paul wrote that ungodly and unrighteous men "exchange the truth of God for a lie" and worship and serve "the creature rather than the Creator" (Rom. 1:25). Robert Girdlestone explained it this way:

"Man is essentially an image-maker. His best works in art and mechanics are imitations of nature....This tendency also shows itself in his religious worship, which he is inclined to make as symbolical as possible. Nay, he seeks to make a sensible representation even of God Himself, and gradually to transfer to the work of his own hands that reverence and dependence which properly belongs to the one living and true God....Idolatry in its first stage is a sort of symbolism; some object is selected to represent the unseen Deity or to set forth one of His attributes; little by little the material image takes the place of the spiritual reality for which it stands, and idolatry ensues, bringing in its train that sensuality which is the sure attendant of every form of materialism;

the highest functions of human nature are thus abnegated, and human life is debased."[1]

Of course, idolatry does not always take the form of a statue or picture made for that specific purpose. Idolatry can take virtually any form. Paul warned Timothy, "But realize this, that in the last days difficult times will come. For men will be lovers of self, lovers of money...lovers of pleasure rather than lovers of God; holding to a form of godliness, although they have denied its power; and avoid such men as these" (2 Tim. 3:1-5). Loving self, money, pleasure—all these are forms of idolatry because they are elevated to a higher position in human affection than God.

We are worshipers by nature; some*one* or some*thing* will be the object of our veneration, even if it is *ourselves*. Either we worship and serve the "one living and true God" or we do not. There is no third option.

IDOLS IN MODERN LIFE

Unfortunately, idolatry is alive and well in our modern world, and by no means is it limited to primitive or even pagan cultures. There are just as many idols—perhaps more—in the industrialized, high-tech and "Christian" West as there are elsewhere. Millions of people worship artificial gods of their own making at altars dedicated to human achievement and self-sufficiency. God is shoved to the sidelines in their headlong pursuit of knowledge, money, pleasure, and possessions. What makes the situation worse is that this idolatry has infected the Church as well. Even many of us believers may be serving idols and not even be aware of it. The question we must ask ourselves is this: Is there any*thing* or any*one* in our life more important to us than God? If the answer is yes, then we are in the grip of idolatry.

One of the most prevalent forms of idolatry in our culture today is covetousness. Paul wrote to the Colossians, "Mortify therefore your members which are upon the earth; fornication, uncleanness, inordinate affection, evil concupiscence, and *covetousness*, which is idolatry" (Col. 3:5 KJV). Another word for "covetousness" is *greed*, and we have already seen how dangerous that was for the Israelites in the wilderness. It is no less dangerous for us.

During the course of my ministry with Mike Bickle in Kansas City, Mike shared a revelation that God had quickened to him concerning covetousness, especially in the area of money.

One day as Mike was reading the story of Solomon, he came to the passage in Second Chronicles 1:7 where God appeared to Solomon and said to him, "Ask what I shall give you." God was offering Solomon anything he desired—a blank check to be filled in by Solomon for whatever he wanted.

It's interesting to note that the previous verse states that Solomon offered to God a thousand burnt offerings. Solomon had lavishly sacrificed to God. It would appear that God did not want to be outdone by Solomon and said, in effect, "You can't outgive Me. Whatever you desire, I'll give you."

Solomon cried out to God for wisdom and knowledge in order to be a better leader and steward over God's people. As Mike was meditating on this, the Holy Spirit said to him that the New Testament contains the same promise. In John 14:14, Jesus said, "If you ask Me anything in My name, I will do it." The Lord said, "Mike, I have left this promise for every generation as a revealer of where their 'heart' is. This generation found it and said, 'Give me prosperity.' They didn't ask for revival, holiness, the lost for their inheritance, etc. But rather money, money, money." How true it is that out of the abundance of the heart the mouth speaks.

It seems to me that the only reason the average pastor or believer wants to see the "ark" returned to God's house is not for the *glory* but for the *gold*. We no longer desire God for Himself, but rather for what He can do for us. We have become lovers of money rather than lovers of God.

Covetousness is at heart selfishness; it is an attitude of craving, of lusting after something. Covetousness says, "I've got to have that," which leads to a single-minded pursuit that becomes more important than anything else. The *object* of our desire is not as important as our *attitude* toward it. It could be the desire for some new clothes, a new job, maybe a new car, or even a new house. None of these are wrong in and of themselves. It is our attitude toward their pursuit that determines whether or not they are objects of covetous desire. James had stern words for this attitude among believers.

> *What is the source of quarrels and conflicts among you? Is not the source your pleasures that wage war in your members? You lust and do not have; so you commit murder. And you are envious and cannot obtain; so you fight and quarrel. You do not have because you do not ask. You ask and do not receive, because you ask with wrong motives, so that you may spend it on your pleasures* (James 4:1-3).

Stubbornness is another form of idolatry. Remember Saul, Israel's first king? God commanded him to totally annihilate the Amalekites, including men, women, children, and all livestock. Saul, however, spared not only the king of the Amalekites but also the best of all the livestock to use as sacrifices to God (see 1 Sam. 15:1-21). Samuel confronted Saul's disobedience with the words, "Hath the Lord as great delight in burnt offerings and sacrifices, as in obeying the voice of the Lord? Behold, to obey is better than sacrifice, and to hearken than the fat of rams. For rebellion is as the sin of witchcraft, and stubbornness is as iniquity and idolatry. Because thou hast rejected the word of the Lord, He hath also rejected thee from being king" (1 Sam. 15:22-23 KJV).

Being stubborn means insisting on doing our own thing, our way, no matter what. The New American Standard uses the word *insubordination* instead of *stubbornness* in verse 23, while the New International Version uses the word *arrogance*. All three words help convey the essence of this attitude. We insist on our own way above God's way. We won't bend or yield no matter how much opposition we face. The Bible sometimes uses the word *stiff-necked* to describe people who think this way.

Even religious practices and traditions can become forms of idolatry. A graphic illustration of this is Israel's worship of the idol "Nehustan." Did I say, "idol"? It was really none other than the brazen serpent that God had commanded Moses to make.

How could this bronze figure have become an idol? It was given by God Himself to His people for their deliverance and revealed His power, love, and compassion toward them. It spoke of forgiveness and cleansing from their sin and rebellion. Gradually, however—little by little, as happened to Lot—Israel began to take their eyes off God and transferred their worship to the brazen serpent. It was hundreds of years later when King Hezekiah had to destroy this "past blessing" because the children of Israel had given it the name "Nehustan" (meaning bronze) and were burning incense to it. It had become an idol and taken the place of God Himself.

How quickly we take our eyes off the Lord and focus on some teaching, doctrine, or even experience. I have had numerous e-mails about the "gold dust" that people have seen. Could this be another "Nehustan"? We need to constantly guard our hearts from anything that eclipses the preeminence of Christ in our lives.

Whenever we become so wrapped up in ritual and in always "doing church" the same way that we begin to lose sight of the Person we are supposed to be worshiping, then our practices and traditions have become idolatrous; they are substitutes for the Lord Himself. Anything that we substitute for Christ is idolatry; it doesn't matter what else we may have going for us. Look at the church in Ephesus, for example. In Revelation 2:1-7 the Lord commended the Ephesian church for many things: their hard work, their commitment to what is right, their intolerance for evil or for false teaching, their perseverance. Yet there was one flaw that overshadowed all the good. "But I have this against you, that you have left your first love. Remember therefore from where you have fallen, and repent and do the deeds you did at first; or else I am coming to you, and will remove your lampstand out of its place—unless you repent" (Rev. 2:4-5). In spite of all the good the church was doing, they no longer loved Christ with supreme devotion—and that was the most important of all. The problem was serious enough that the church faced judgment unless they repented.

Idolatry is something that all of us need to look at very, very carefully. We must ask the Lord to show us if there is anything we value more than Him and to reveal any areas in our lives where we may be guilty of idolatry.

Matthew 6:21 says that where our treasure is, there our heart will be also. What do you treasure or cherish? What is the focus of your love? Anything other than God that takes the center of your attention and value is an idol. When you give God all your heart, you will truly fall in love with Him. Genuine love for God is the cure for idolatry. A passion for Him makes all other loves seem shallow in comparison.

We need to be able to say, "God, I don't want to have any other gods before You. I don't want my god to be my house, my car, my job, my family, or anything else. I don't want anything to consume me. Instead, I want to be consumed with You." If we don't, we will be laid low in the wilderness and miss out on God's purpose.

Mingling With the Nations

Another deadly sin that laid Israel low in the wilderness was immorality. Paul writes, "Nor let us act immorally, as some of them did, and twenty-three thousand fell in one day" (1 Cor. 10:8). The incident that Paul refers to here is what Second Peter 2:15 calls the "way of Balaam," and Jude 11 the "error of Balaam." Revelation 2:14 warns the church in Pergamum, "I have a few things against you, because you have there some who hold the teaching of Balaam, who kept teaching Balak to put a stumbling block before the sons of Israel, to eat things sacrificed to idols, and to commit acts of immorality."

Balaam was a Mesopotamian prophet hired by Balak, king of Moab, to curse the Israelites. (Remember, Moab was a descendant of Lot!) Through this, Balak hoped to defeat Israel in battle. The story is found in chapters 22 through 24 of the Book of Numbers. Three times Balak implored Balaam to curse Israel. Three times Balaam responded that he could speak only what the Lord gave him to speak. Three times Balaam spoke words of blessing over Israel from the Lord. Balaam was unable to curse Israel or to get the Lord to do so. However, according to Revelation 2:14, Balaam apparently told Balak how to get the Israelites to bring a curse upon themselves; he told the king to seduce the Israelites into idolatry and immorality. The story of this tragic development is recounted Numbers 25.

> *While Israel remained at Shittim, the people began to play the harlot with the daughters of Moab. For they invited the people to the sacrifices of their gods, and the people ate and bowed down to their gods. So Israel joined themselves to Baal of Peor, and the Lord was angry against Israel....And those who died by the plague were 24,000* (Numbers 25:1-3,9).

God's plan and desire was to bless Israel and make them a great and prosperous nation. Israel, however, brought God's curse upon themselves through their lack of self-control. The Moabites invited the Israelites to join in the sacrifices, festivals, and worship of Baal, which involved ritual prostitution as well as eating food that had been offered to their gods. Unable to control themselves (and perhaps unwilling to do so) the Israelites yielded to the temptation, committed idolatry and acts of immorality, and brought God's curse upon themselves.

The sorry scene with the Moabites is a powerful illustration of the danger of compromise. God wanted His people to be completely separate from the pagan nations around them as far as sin, righteousness, and religious practice were concerned. Israel's disregard in this matter was one of their earliest compromises. One compromise led to another, then another, in a descending cycle toward disaster. (Read Psalm 106, which recounts the complete history of Israel in the wilderness.)

The Israelites' failure to drive out or exterminate the pagan peoples in Canaan led to mingling with them. Mingling resulted in Israel's learning the ways of the pagans, which led to their adopting practices of gross idolatry and immorality. The Israelites even sank so low as to practice human sacrifice. It all began with mingling, with compromise. It's always easier to be dragged down to someone else's level than it is to raise that person up to ours.

Winkie Pratney has adapted a poem that speaks to the Church's tendency toward compromise with the world:

THE CHURCH AND THE WORLD

"The Church and the World walked far apart on the changing
    shores of time
And the World was singing a charts rock tune, but the Church a
    hymn sublime
'Come, give me your hand' called the laid-back world 'and dance
    with me this day'

But the love-cleansed Church hid her blood-bought hand and
    solemnly said 'No way'
'I will not give you my hand at all, and I will not walk with you
Your way is the way of Eternal Death and your words are all
    untrue'
'Ah, walk with me! Just a little way' said the World with insistent
    air
'The space I'm at is a pleasant place, and the night-life is magic
    there
You've been battling with me for far too long, and let's face it,
    you've been so alone
Don't you think it high time that we called a truce, and you found
    some place here for a home
Your life is so narrow and thorny and tough' see how mine runs
    so easy and smooth
Why be so repressive and out of it? In the finest of circles I
    move....
My way, you see, is a fun, fast one, and my gate is so broad and
    so wide
There is room enough for you and me to travel it side by side....

'Half shyly the Church approached the world, and gave him her
    hand of snow
And the fake world grasped it and drew her close, and whispered
    in accents low—
'Your dress is too simple to please my taste. I've got all kinds of
    things you can wear
See these silks and chiffons and synthetic stones and this dazzling
    disco gear?
The Church looked down at her plain white robes, and then at the
    glittering world
And blushed as she saw his superstar style and his smile con-
    temptuous curled
'I can change my dress' she said to him 'After all, I am under
    grace'
And her pure white garments were stripped away, and the World
    gave her wealth in their place
'Now your house is passe' said the proud grey World 'Let me
    build you a place like mine

With a barbecue pit for the parties we'll throw and a mirrow-tiled
    bedroom so fine....
So the parties began and the dancing went on in the place that was
    once made for prayer
And the Church felt relief that the battle was over and that she at
    last has no care....

But an angel of mercy flew over the Church and whispered 'I
    know thy sin'....
Then the Church looked up, and anxiously tried to gather her chil-
    dren in
But some were down at the discotheque, and others were off at
    play
And some were drinking in gay night bars, so she quietly went her
    way
Then the sly world gallantly said to her 'Your children mean no
    harm
Just having "some fun" he said and he smiled, so she took his
    proffered arm
And smiled, and went back to gathering flowers, as she chattered
    and walked with the World
While millions and millions of precious souls to the horrible pit
    were hurled

'There are preachers you have that bother me' said the world with
    a contemporary sneer
It seems they keep trying to frighten my kids with tales that I
    don't want them to hear—
They talk about "sinning" and "breaking God's heart" and this
    horror of "endless night"
And the awful rude way they reject my suggestions is terribly
    impolite—
Now I have some men of a much better breed, contemporary, bril-
    liant and fast
Who can show us all how we can live as we like and go to Nir-
    vana at last....
The Infinite Spirit is within us all, and is peaceful, enlightened
    and kind—
Do you think It would take one child to Itself and leave any other
    behind?

Go, train up your speakers to fit with the times, adopt to the rele-
    vant way
Everyone likes entertainment today, and it's only the good shows
    that pay.'

So she called for those of the swift repartee', the gifted, flamboy-
    ant and learned
While plain good men who had preached the cross were out of
    their pulpits turned
Then the Church sat down in her ease and said 'I am rich and in
    goods increased
I have nothing I need and nothing to do but to laugh and to dance
    and to feast'
And the sly World heard her and laughed within, and mockingly
    said aside—
'The Church has fallen, the beautiful Church, and her shame is
    her boast and her pride'

And an angel drew near the mercy seat, and whispered in sighs
    her name
And the saints their anthems of rapture hushed, and covered their
    heads with shame
And a voice came down from the hush of Heaven, from Him who
    sat on the throne—
'I know your works and what you have said and I know that you
    have not known
You are poor and blind and naked and sick, with pride and ruin
    enthralled
The expectant Bride of a heavenly Groom, now the Hooker of all
    the world
You have ceased to watch for your Saviours return and have fall-
    en from zeal and grace
So now, in tears, I must cast you out and BLOT OUT YOUR
    NAME FROM ITS PLACE.'[2]

THE WAY OF BALAAM

One of the greatest challenges for the Church in any generation is to
aggressively engage the world with the message of Christ without being
seduced or corrupted by the ways of the world. There is a right way and a
wrong way to mingle with the world. The right way is the way of holiness—to

walk as the "salt of the earth" and the "light of the world" with a bold and unapologetic testimony for Christ. The wrong way is the way of compromise, the way of accommodation with the world; a way that seeks at all cost to avoid offense.

I recall hearing Corrie ten Boom contrast the difference between thermometers and thermostats. She said that a thermometer changes according to the temperature of its surroundings. However, a thermostat remains fixed regardless of the conditions around it. In her own unique way, she said that too many Christians are like thermometers, changing to whatever conditions they find themselves in. What we need, she said, is Christians who, like thermostats, remain the same regardless of what is going on around them. Jesus said, "I do not ask Thee to take them out of the world, but to keep them from the evil..." (Jn. 17:15).

When Israel followed the way of Balaam, God had no choice but to bring judgment upon them. God must judge sin; He can neither ignore it nor excuse it. The Israelites took for granted their status as the "chosen people." They thought that they were so blessed of God that they could do anything and get away with it. They were God's children, so sin would not hurt them. That was a deadly deception and one of the subtleties of the way of Balaam.

One way the enemy deceives us is getting us to think that God isn't concerned about the sin in our life because His blessings are continuing. So we continue in our sin. What we have done is believed the lie of the enemy that God understands our "weakness" and, therefore, makes concessions for our sin. Nothing could be further from the truth. The fact is that God is not condoning sin, but rather, in His infinite love toward us, allowing us time to repent. We should never confuse His patience with His approval. A classic example is that of Jezebel in the Book of Revelation, chapter 2. This so-called prophetess was teaching "her flock" that immorality was okay—no doubt under a misunderstanding of grace or eternal security. The Scriptures make clear that God was totally opposed to her teaching; yet, it said she was given time to repent. In her case God's patience ultimately comes to an end, and, because of her refusal to repent, she is killed along with her "children."

Many in the Church today are in danger of following the way of Balaam. Many others have already succumbed. If we are not careful, we can develop an attitude that says, "I am a child of God, blessed of the Father and secure in Christ. No man can separate me from the love of Christ or take me out of the Father's hand, so I can get by with sin; it won't hurt me." Yes, it will. That is the attitude of compromise. It is an attitude that winks at sin and neither understands nor takes seriously the principles of holiness and righteousness.

Immorality—the way of Balaam—is rampant today in the Body of Christ. The moral relativism of our society has influenced even the attitudes of many believers. The tragedy is that many Christians, particularly young people, are confused or ignorant as to what constitutes godly and moral attitudes and behavior. Many children, even "church kids," are sexually active now as young as the age of 11. Premarital sex has become such a norm in the dating world that it is almost expected. In many parts of the country, especially in some of our largest cities, condoms are handed out like candy. This current generation is absolutely obsessed with sex. We are confronted with it everywhere we turn in books, magazines, movies, and television shows.

Consider this example. One morning in the summer of 1999 I picked up my copy of "The Pastor's Weekly Briefing" published by Focus on the Family. In it, under "The News at a Glance," was the following:

"The Presbyterian Church (U.S.A.) general assembly voted Wednesday in support of revising their education curriculum to include a more abstinence-based stance. The current program teaches abstinence and also offers contraceptives."

The incidence of Christian ministers falling because of moral failure continues to rise and gets worse every day. One of the newest, subtlest, and most seductive threats to ministers (as well as to other believers) is pornography on the Internet. The threat is so real, in fact, that the Assemblies of God sent a personal letter to its ministers warning pastors about the temptation of Internet pornography. Anything goes where the Internet is concerned. Virtually anything can be found there. It is very easy for a pastor today to get addicted to pornography while sitting in his office. Everything is right there on the Internet. If someone walks into the office, a simple click of the mouse removes all the evidence. Internet pornography is pervasive, seductive, and dangerous.

I know personally a minister in New Zealand who fell into disgrace because of illicit sexual affairs. This man had been a leader for years in his denomination. A man of passion, he had helped his denomination move from a small, sleepy group to a major movement and had built one of the largest churches in New Zealand. He attracted a lot of young people and inspired and built a major organization. He was an excellent administrator and a seasoned pastor. Now he's gone, brought down because he succumbed to the way of Balaam and failed to exercise self-control.

KNOWN BY OUR FRUITS

Not only the leaders, but also the whole Body of Christ is being assaulted by the demonic hordes that promote lust and seduce individuals into all forms of deviant behavior. Many Christians are just as confused as anyone else regarding proper behavior and are just as prone to fall into sin. Somewhere along the way we have lost our moral compass. The world is looking for the Church to display true attributes of holiness and righteousness. We need to be absolutely clear about who we are and how we are to live. Jesus said, "For there is no good tree which produces bad fruit; nor, on the other hand, a bad tree which produces good fruit. For each tree is known by its own fruit. For men do not gather figs from thorns, nor do they pick grapes from a briar bush" (Lk. 6:43-44).

We will be known by the fruit in our lives, whether it be the fruit of the flesh or the fruit of the Spirit. Which fruit we bear depends on whether we indulge the flesh or embrace the Spirit. Indulging the flesh leads to such "fruit" as "immorality, impurity, sensuality, idolatry, sorcery, enmities, strife, jealousy, outbursts of anger, disputes, dissensions, factions, envying, drunkenness, [and] carousing" (Gal. 5:19b-21a). On the other hand, embracing the Spirit brings to bear in our lives the fruit of "love, joy, peace, patience, kindness, goodness, faithfulness, gentleness, [and] self-control" (Gal. 5:22b-23a).

We live in a world where it is frightfully easy to discover too late that we have been "sleeping with the enemy." How can we evaluate ourselves and know not only who we are but also how to live faithfully as believers in a sinful and seductive environment? In his book, *That Incredible Christian*, A.W. Tozer lists seven tests for such self-judgment:

- What we want most.
- What we think about most.
- How we use our money.
- What we do with our leisure time.
- The company we enjoy.
- Whom and what we admire.
- What we laugh at.[3]

Evaluating ourselves by these criteria in the light of the Word of God will help us better understand ourselves and our motivation. What do we want more than anything else in the world? What do we think about voluntarily? What do we do with our discretionary money? How do we spend our free time? Who do we "hang" with? Who do we look to as examples and models? Does our sense of humor honor God or cater to the world?

We *will* be known by our fruits. What does your fruit say about your life? Does it show you to be a child of the world or a child of the King, in training for residence and rule in Zion, the great city of God?

ENDNOTES

1. Robert Baker Girdlestone, *Synonyms of the Old Testament* (Grand Rapids, Michigan: Wm. B. Eerdmans Publishing Company, n.d.), 303.

2. "The Church and the World," author unknown (adopted from original by W.A. Pratney). Used by permission. Reprinted as is.

3. A.W. Tozer, *That Incredible Christian* (Camp Hill, Pennsylvania: Christian Publications, Inc., n.d.), 102-103.

Chapter Six

Marching to Zion

HOW could Israel ever forget this incredible sight as they stood there on the banks of the Red Sea? They watched the entire Egyptian army being swallowed up by the mighty torrents of water cascading down upon them. God was unleashing His mighty hand of judgment against those who had helped impose Israel's forced captivity of oppression and slavery.

The people could hardly contain their excitement as Miriam grabbed her tambourine and began dancing for joy over her newfound freedom. No longer would she and her people be enslaved to taskmasters who daily made their lives unbearable. This was the freedom God's people had waited for. Miriam challenged the people to magnify the Lord with her for His deliverance on their behalf.

As wonderful as this experience was, it was merely the beginning—the first step in God's plan and purpose for His people. Even as they celebrated, God had His goal in mind—to "bring them and plant them in the mountain of [His] inheritance" (Ex. 15:17a). His purpose was to have a people passionately in love with Him, a people who shared His heart for others who were still in slavery and bondage. What better way to reach other oppressed people than to have a nation testifying to their miraculous deliverance from bondage because of God's supernatural grace and mercy freely shown to them.

This, then, was the first stage in God's plan to bring Israel *out* of their bondage; through the wilderness of testing, growth, and preparation; and *into* the land of promise, where they would dwell in the very presence of God. This divine habitation is known by several names in the Bible, one of the most common of which is *Zion*. God's plan was to bring His people into

Zion and establish them in a life that revolved around His presence. It was a place of joy, celebration, and authority; a place that would show all people His love, presence, and fellowship.

The same thing is true for the Church. Christ redeemed us when He died on the cross. He bought us with His own blood to make us His own special possession. But His ultimate goal is to gather *all nations* to Himself.

In my first book, *For God's Sake, Grow Up!*, I cover in greater detail the message of the true meaning of the cross. I'm convinced after 35 years of ministry that we have little real understanding of why Christ died. We often view the atoning work of Calvary only from our perspective. When is the last time you heard the cross from God's perspective? We preach that Christ died for our sake, never thinking about what *God* derives from His Son's suffering and death.

This is a whole study in itself, but allow me to mention one verse: Revelation 5:9. "Worthy art Thou to take the book, and to break its seals; for Thou wast slain, *and didst purchase for God with Thy blood men* from every tribe and tongue and people and nation." From this verse alone we see that God had more in mind than simply man's forgiveness; He was putting a claim of ownership on our lives.

One illustration I have used for years is the analogy of buying a used car. After months of work, I finally had $1,000 saved. Since I was without transport of my own, I decided to buy a vehicle. After days of searching for a suitable car for the price, I found and bought a 15-year-old car. Needless to say, the car was not exactly in showroom condition. But I was determined to do my best to make it so. After hours and hours of work, I had before me a transformed car. Everything was clean and sparkling. Not only had I washed the car, but I also had polished it to make it look like new. Imagine my wife's reaction if I had taken all the cleaning stuff into the house and piled it on the table—a bucket of filthy water; rags and towels used for washing, drying, and polishing; and the contents of the vacuum cleaner. "Look, darling, this is what I bought for $1,000." Now, while my purchase did include the dirt, that was not my purpose in buying. The *car* was the object of my payment. Likewise, when Jesus Christ suffered as the final sacrifice for sin, it was *you* He had in mind. "Do you not know that…you are not your own? For *you* have been bought [cross] with a price…" (1 Cor. 6:19-20).

Writing to Titus, Paul said that it was Christ "who gave Himself for us, that He might redeem us from every lawless deed and purify for Himself a people for His own possession, zealous for good deeds" (Tit. 2:14). In the same vein Peter wrote, "But you are a chosen race, a royal priesthood, a holy nation, a people for God's own possession, that you may proclaim the excellencies of Him who has called you out of darkness into His marvelous light"

(1 Pet. 2:9). In both Israel and the Church God was looking for a people totally given over to His will and purpose, a people whom He could bring into "the mountain of [His] inheritance," that is, into Zion.

ZION: THE CITY OF DAVID

Historically and geographically Zion is associated with the city of Jerusalem. Originally the name of a fortified hill located between the Kidron and Tyropean valleys, Zion is the oldest part of Jerusalem. The first scriptural appearance of the name *Zion* occurs in relation to David's capture of Jerusalem. At that time the city and the fortified stronghold of Zion were inhabited by a people known as the Jebusites, who had been there for centuries. The Jebusites were one of several tribes of people living in Canaan whom the Israelites had never been successful in driving out (see Josh. 15:63; Judg. 1:21).

Nevertheless, David defeated the Jebusites, occupied Zion, moved his personal residence there, and renamed it "the city of David." In this way the names "Zion" and "City of David" became synonymous. Soon after this, Jerusalem became the religious center of the nation and began to develop great spiritual significance in the hearts and minds of the Hebrew people. First, the ark of the covenant was moved there, so the city became associated with God's presence. Second, it was in Jerusalem that God made an everlasting covenant with the house of David: "And your house and your kingdom shall endure before Me forever; your throne shall be established forever" (2 Sam. 7:16). Third, after David's death his son Solomon built the magnificent temple that David had dreamed of. Once the ark of the covenant was placed in the Holy of Holies, the temple became an even more powerful reminder to the people of God's presence among them.[1]

Jerusalem, then, was seen as *the dwelling place of Israel's kings, through which the nation gradually came to appreciate and celebrate the kingship of God*, one of the central themes of the Bible.[2] This understanding is expressed throughout the Psalms; many psalms extol the various characteristics, both physical and spiritual, of Jerusalem.

> *Great is the Lord, and greatly to be praised, in the city of our God, His holy mountain. Beautiful in elevation, the joy of the whole earth, is Mount Zion in the far north, the city of the great King* (Psalm 48:1-2).

> *God is known in Judah; His name is great in Israel. And His tabernacle is in Salem; His dwelling place also is in Zion* (Psalm 76:1-2).

For the Lord has chosen Zion; He has desired it for His habita-
tion. "This is My resting place forever; here I will dwell, for I
have desired it" (Psalm 132:13-14).

Zion, the city of David, is also the city of God.

ZION: THE CITY OF MELCHIZEDEK

Centuries before David, even centuries before Moses, Jerusalem
appears in Scripture for the first time in relation to an event in Abram's life.
Abram has just returned from his successful campaign to free his nephew
Lot from the coalition of kings and armies that had taken him.

And Melchizedek king of Salem brought out bread and wine; now
he was a priest of God Most High. And he blessed him and said,
"Blessed be Abram of God Most High, possessor of heaven and
earth; and blessed be God Most High, who has delivered your
enemies into your hand." And he gave him a tenth of all (Genesis
14:18-20).

"It would seem that Melchizedek built the original city of
Jerusalem....The word Jerusalem is made up of two words and
the term 'Jeru' signifies a foundation of righteousness and the
word 'salem' signifies peace."[3]

I believe Abraham, "the father of all who believe," was made to understand that *God's ultimate calling was to have, like Melchizedek, a company*
of kings and priests ministering and reigning from "Zion" or Jerusalem.
Melchizedek is without a doubt one of the most mysterious and tanta-
lizing figures in the Bible. He appears out of nowhere, blesses Abram, and
calls Abram "possessor of heaven and earth." This blessing is similar to
God's promise to Abram: "I will greatly multiply your seed as the stars of
the heavens, and as the sand which is on the seashore" (Gen. 22:17b). In
response to this blessing Abram gives Melchizedek a tithe (a tenth) of his
spoil from the battle. Apart from this reference, Melchizedek is mentioned
in Scripture only in Psalm 110:4 and in the Book of Hebrews. These references, though few, nevertheless tell us some important things.

First, Melchizedek was "king of Salem." Salem was a very early name
for Jerusalem. Hebrews 7:2 says that the name *Melchizedek* means "king of
righteousness," and that "king of Salem" means "king of peace." Second,
Melchizedek was "a priest of the Most High God." Like Abram, Melchizedek worshiped and served the one living and true God. By giving him
a tenth of the spoils Abram acknowledged Melchizedek's priesthood. So
Melchizedek was both king and priest.

Centuries later the Jewish priesthood would be established through the tribe of Levi with Aaron as the first high priest. According to the Mosaic Law, priests were to come only from the Levitical line. King David was from the tribe of Judah, and it was to him that God made the promise to establish his royal line forever. Kings were kings and priests were priests; under the Jewish system no one person could fill both functions. Yet Psalm 110, clearly a messianic psalm, says of the Messiah (who would be a king descended from David's line), "Thou art a priest forever according to the order of Melchizedek" (Ps. 110:4b). The writer of the Book of Hebrews, referring to this verse, plainly states that "Jesus has entered as a forerunner for us, having become a high priest forever according to the order of Melchizedek" (Heb. 6:20). Melchizedek was "without father, without mother, without genealogy, having neither beginning of days nor end of life, but made like the Son of God, he abides a priest perpetually" (Heb. 7:3). The writer goes on to demonstrate that the priesthood of Melchizedek is superior to the Levitical priesthood because it is based not on "a law of physical requirement, but according to the power of an indestructible life" (Heb. 7:16b). That "indestructible life" is Christ.

Melchizedek, then, is a biblical "type" of Christ, one who is both priest and king and whose offices endure forever. He represents a heavenly priesthood that is greater and more perfect than the earthly priesthood that came through Levi. So even from its earliest appearance in Scripture Jerusalem (Salem, Zion) is linked with God's redemptive purpose to raise up "a chosen race, a royal priesthood, a holy nation, a people for God's own possession" (1 Pet. 2:9a) and bring them into His habitation.

ZION: THE CITY OF DIVINE GOVERNMENT

As the capital city of the nation of Israel, *Jerusalem was at the very heart of Jewish national and religious identity*. The king's palace was there, and from it went forth his laws and decrees. During the reigns of David and Solomon in particular, Jerusalem was built up and expanded into a very beautiful city. When the queen of Sheba visited Solomon she was impressed not only by his wisdom but also by the immensity of his wealth. The king's prosperity was a reflection of the prosperity of the city and the nation.

Jerusalem was the focal point for the spiritual life of the people. The temple, planned and prepared for by David and built by Solomon, was the centerpiece of everyday religious life and practice. It permeated the people's very existence. As the dwelling place of God, the Temple defined in a tangible way the Israelites' concept of who they were and of their uniqueness as God's chosen people. They saw the rule of God issuing forth from Jerusalem just as surely as they saw the king's decrees.

Zion was the city of the Lord, the great King, and was the place of His power, authority, and government. It was the place of Heaven's rule, the place where God's will was revealed. Part of God's purpose for Israel was that they be a center of righteousness and holiness from which God's rule would spread throughout the earth, touching all peoples and races.

By extension in the New Testament age, *Zion* applies to the Church. Just as with Israel, God's purpose for the Church is that we be the spiritual authority through which Christ can reign and rule; that we proclaim salvation by grace through faith in Christ; that we bind and loose; that we cast out demons; and that the gates of hell do not prevail against us. His desire is for the Church to demonstrate the power and authority of God. Paul and Silas were described as "men who have upset the world" (Acts 17:6b). Does the world say the same thing about us? Are the power and authority of God on display in the Church today?

The Bible clearly teaches that "all Scripture is inspired by God and profitable for teaching…training…" etc. (2 Tim. 3:16). Therefore, the Scriptures have both a past application and a present application. We are also told in the Word that first comes the natural, and then the spiritual (see 1 Cor. 15:46).

With this in mind, I believe "Zion" had both a past application to Israel, but also contains a prophetic application for the Church. The writer to Hebrews makes this abundantly clear when he writes to the early believers in these words, "But you have come to Mount Zion and to the city of the living God, the heavenly Jerusalem…to the general assembly and church of the first-born…." (Heb. 12:22-23).

There is no doubt in my mind that what we see in natural Zion reveals God's purpose for the citizens of spiritual Zion. We are told prophetically that "the latter glory of this house will be greater than the former" (Hag. 2:9). Everything addressed to the Hebrews was prefaced by the word *better,* not *lesser.* May God open our eyes to His purpose for the present Zion—us, His people.

Zion was a place of instruction. In addition to expressing the power and authority of God, Israel was also to know God, learn His ways, and teach those ways to others. The people needed to be taught how to approach God with reverence and fear and how to walk in the way of holiness and righteousness.

And now, Israel, what does the Lord your God require from you,
but to fear the Lord your God, to walk in all His ways and love

Him, and to serve the Lord your God with all your heart and with all your soul, and to keep the Lord's commandments and His statutes which I am commanding you today for your good? (Deuteronomy 10:12-13)

And many peoples will come and say, "Come, let us go up to the mountain of the Lord, to the house of the God of Jacob; that He may teach us concerning His ways, and that we may walk in His paths." For the law will go forth from Zion, and the word of the Lord from Jerusalem (Isaiah 2:3).

In the same way the Church is to have deep knowledge of God and His ways. The Word of God is our textbook and the Holy Spirit our Teacher. God's law is to go forth from our lips and our lives, not the "law of sin and of death" but the "law of the Spirit of life in Christ Jesus" (Rom. 8:2).

Ancient Zion was a fortress that towered above everything around it. The Psalmist describes it as "beautiful in elevation, the joy of the whole earth" (Ps. 48:2). Likewise, God desires a people of stature, magnificent and majestic in character—His showpiece to the world. Everything about our lives should reflect His nature and Christlikeness. We are to be His witnesses, His light, and His workmanship. We are not simply to *know* His Word; He wants the Word to be made flesh in us so men can see and read our lives. We are epistles, written and read of all men, according to Paul (see 2 Cor. 3:2). Do our lives cause others to want more? Do they want to turn the page, so to speak, in anticipation of learning more? Or do they turn away, saying, "That (epistle) book doesn't interest me"? Floyd McClung of Youth With a Mission used to say, "People don't care how much we know. They want to know how much we care." Let's let our lives shine.

ZION: THE CITY OF WARFARE

If Zion represents the center of God's power, authority, government, and knowledge, then it also is a prime target for enemy attack. Satan sets his sights on any individual, church, or other group that stands boldly for righteousness, morality, and the Kingdom of Heaven. A world at odds with God squirms and resists what it sees as the restraints put upon it by the demands of God's laws. The words of Psalm 2 express it well:

Why are the nations in an uproar, and the peoples devising a vain thing? The kings of the earth take their stand, and the rulers take counsel together against the Lord and against His Anointed: "Let us tear their fetters apart, and cast away their cords from us!" (Psalm 2:1-3)

This is exactly what has happened throughout history. Time after time different nations rose up against Israel, only to end up defeated and destroyed. On the other hand, when the nation of Israel sinned, God allowed them to be defeated by their enemies. Even so, God later judged and brought down those nations He had used to judge Israel.

Jesus felt the full brunt of the fury, rage, and hatred of the rulers of the people aroused against Him. They hated Jesus because He exposed the wickedness of their hearts and the rebelliousness of their spirits toward God. The early Church faced severe persecution for boldly proclaiming Christ. Many believers paid with their lives.

The same thing is happening today. More Christians have died for their faith in the twentieth century than in any other century in history. In fact, it is probably not a stretch to say that more Christians have been martyred in this century than in all other centuries *combined*. Less than a year ago we saw the nation reel in horror and disgust at what happened at Columbine High School in Littleton, Colorado. Two students opened fire on their fellow students. When their rampage of death and destruction was over, 15 people lay dead and 23 others wounded. The nation mourned for weeks. Among the dead were teens who had openly declared their faith in God. Another who was wounded but survived the shooting likewise testified to her love for Christ. The story is told that one victim, Rachel Scott, was lying wounded when one of the gunmen approached her and asked, "Do you believe in God?" When she replied, "Yes," he said, "Then go be with Him," and shot her through the temple.

What does the twenty-first century hold?

I believe the day is coming when the Church will be singled out for attack to a degree greater than ever before. The spiritual warfare will be unlike anything we have ever seen. In many ways it is already happening. Satan has a full arsenal of weapons that we must constantly guard against: division, compromise, worldliness, apathy, lethargy, pride…the list could go on. It is possible that the Church could become the last bastion of restraint; the last stronghold for righteousness, morality, and integrity; the only institution standing in the way of the world's having the freedom to do whatever it wants. The world will say, "We're bound by the fetters of the Church. They are too restrictive; they are restraining us. Let's break those bonds and cast them away! We need to be free!"

The Church will come under constant attack, not only from spiritual powers and principalities, but also from the world itself. Jesus told us this would be the case. "If the world hates you, you know that it has hated Me before it hated you" (Jn. 15:18). "These things I have spoken to you, that in

Me you may have peace. In the world you have tribulation, but take courage; I have overcome the world" (Jn. 16:33).

Even as the hatred and opposition of the world increase, so too will the grace, power, and protection of God over His people. Jesus promised peace and overcoming in the midst of tribulation. Psalm 2 also speaks of the overcoming of the Lord's enemies.

> *"But as for Me, I have installed My King upon Zion, My holy mountain." I will surely tell of the decree of the Lord: He said to Me, 'Thou art My Son, today I have begotten Thee. Ask of Me, and I will surely give the nations as Thine inheritance, and the very ends of the earth as Thy possession. Thou shalt break them with a rod of iron, Thou shalt shatter them like earthenware.' Now therefore, O kings, show discernment; take warning, O judges of the earth. Worship the Lord with reverence, and rejoice with trembling. Do homage to the Son, lest He become angry, and you perish in the way, for His wrath may soon be kindled. How blessed are all who take refuge in Him!* (Psalm 2:6-12)

Just as God established His king on ancient Zion, so He will establish Zion in these last days. In fact, He is already doing it in His Church.

ZION IN THE PURPOSE OF GOD

God has a marvelous plan, a destiny for His people. That plan involves dwelling forever in Zion. God dwells in Zion, and He wants His people to dwell there too in His everlasting presence. Part of God's purpose, then, is for Zion to be the everlasting possession of His people. *Zion is the place of God's affection.* "The Lord loves the gates of Zion more than all the other dwelling places of Jacob" (Ps. 87:2).

When speaking of Zion, we must be careful to point out that God's purpose is to be realized here and now, in the present, and not simply in the future. Most believers know that eventually everything will "pan out" okay, but they lose sight of the fact that God wants a triumphant Church now as well. Jesus gave us the promise that He would build His Church and that the gates of hell would not prevail against it (see Mt. 16:18).

Zion is no longer a geographical location but a spiritual position—we are the "Zion" of God. We are His holy habitation, the delight of His heart, the object of His affections, the place of His presence and power. (Or perhaps I should say that we have the *potential* to be all this.)

Zion is the victory of God's people. "And the sons of those who afflicted you will come bowing to you, and all those who despised you will bow themselves at the soles of your feet; and they will call you the city of the Lord, the Zion of the Holy One of Israel" (Is. 60:14). This speaks of victory over every evil foe. What God desired for Israel He desires for the Church. God's purpose is for the Church to live in victory.

Victory does not necessarily mean that we live free from problems, trials, and difficulties, but that we triumph *in* these difficult and trying circumstances. There may be times when God removes these problems and there may be times when He supplies the grace to go through them.

Few Christians have not admired Joni Erickson Tada. Her natural beauty has not eclipsed the beauty of Christ that she expresses constantly even though she is confined to a wheelchair. Truly, she has triumphed through tragedy and risen from victim to victor.

Zion is the joy of God's people. There is great joy in the presence of God for all who love Him. "Cry aloud and shout for joy, O inhabitant of Zion, for great in your midst is the Holy One of Israel" (Is. 12:6). "And though you have not seen Him, you love Him, and though you do not see Him now, but believe in Him, you greatly rejoice with joy inexpressible and full of glory" (1 Pet. 1:8).

The world needs to see what true joy is all about. Many people confuse joy and happiness. They are not the same. Happiness is a state of mind that depends greatly on external circumstances (happenings). As long as we feel good, or things are going our way, we feel happy. Joy goes much deeper; its source is in God. It is a deep, unshakable sense of well-being and delight that comes from being in the presence of God and from the assurance that we are right with God. Thus joy does not depend on externals. Paul and Silas in the Philippian jail were filled with joy despite their grim, dirty, and unhappy surroundings. Their joy was not affected by their chains because it did not depend on their circumstances.

God wants His people to be joyful. Jesus said, "These things I have spoken to you, that My joy may be in you, and that your joy may be made full" (Jn. 15:11). A joy-filled Church is a powerful witness to a joy-starved world. Acts says of the disciples "...the disciples were continually filled with joy and with the Holy Spirit" (Acts 13:52).

Zion is the testimony of God's people; it is a place of witness. "For Zion's sake I will not keep silent, and for Jerusalem's sake I will not keep quiet, until her righteousness goes forth like brightness, and her salvation like a torch that is burning. And the nations will see your righteousness, and all kings your glory" (Is. 62:1-2a). This was fulfilled literally in Solomon's day when the kings of the earth came to Jerusalem to hear the wisdom of Solomon and to see the beauty of God's house and the splendor of the city.

With her righteousness "like brightness" and her salvation like "a torch that is burning," Zion was to be a light to the nations, revealing God and His ways to the peoples of the earth. John the Baptist epitomized this purpose. The biblical record reveals him as "the lamp that was burning and was shining," and men rejoiced in his light (Jn. 5:35). This rugged, radical revolutionary was ablaze with the Spirit of God. His very life became the message: He was "the lamp that was burning."

Jesus said, "I have come to cast fire on the earth." Not the fire of judgment, but the fire of the Holy Spirit as on the Day of Pentecost. On that day men were transformed from fearful failures to mighty fervent flames that caused people to be drawn to their brightness.

In the tabernacle and later the temple, the golden lampstand held a constant flame of fire. One of the responsibilities of the priest was to, morning and evening, trim the lamps so that the flame remained intense and undimmed.

In the New Testament we see the great high priest Jesus Christ Himself walking among the seven lampstands (churches) inspecting and trimming their lights or witness. He seeks to reprove or remove from His Church those areas that hinder their witness to the world. The Church is, very simply, His people. However, what is true corporately is also true individually. Like the ten virgins of old, we need to have our lights trimmed. Paul had to rebuke the Romans for their lifestyle. He told them that they dishonored God. "The name of God is blasphemed among the Gentiles [heathen] because of you" (see Rom. 2:24). Jesus exhorted us to "let your light shine before men in such a way that they may see your good works, and glorify your Father who is in heaven" (Mt. 5:16). How attractive is your light?

Israel was to be a holy nation as a witness to the world of a holy God. "Awake, awake, clothe yourself in your strength, O Zion; clothe yourself in your beautiful garments, O Jerusalem, the holy city. For the uncircumcised and the unclean will no more come into you" (Is. 52:1).

The ultimate purpose of Zion in the Old Testament was to show us what the Church is to be like in the New Testament. By extension, the Church is the spiritual Zion. Like the nation of Israel, the Church is to be a light to the nations, "a chosen race, a royal priesthood, a holy nation, a people for God's own possession" (1 Pet. 2:9a) that we may shine His light in a sin-darkened world. This requires a radical commitment to holiness on the part of every believer. "But like the Holy One who called you, be holy yourselves also in all your behavior; because it is written, 'You shall be holy, for I am holy' " (1 Pet. 1:15-16).

Zion is the security of God's people. Since preDavidic times Zion has been a fortress, a stronghold. Within its walls (both literally and figuratively) the children of God find protection and safety. We are secure because Zion is the place of God's presence. "Jerusalem will be inhabited without walls, because of the multitude of men and cattle within it. 'For I,' declares the Lord, 'will be a wall of fire around her, and I will be the glory in her midst' " (Zech. 2:4b-5).

Thank God for His promise to abide with us today and dwell within us: "I will never leave thee, nor forsake thee" (Heb. 13:5b KJV). What incredible strength and security is to be found in these promises. "Lo, I am with you always" (Mt. 28:20).

Zion is the unity of God's people. For the nation of Israel, Zion was where all the tribes came together to worship God. Psalm 133 is a "psalm of ascents," one of a series of psalms that were sung by Israelites as they made the pilgrimage up to Jerusalem to worship. It speaks of unity among God's people.

> *Behold, how good and how pleasant it is for brothers to dwell together in unity! It is like the precious oil upon the head, coming down upon the beard, even Aaron's beard, coming down upon the edge of his robes. It is like the dew of Hermon, coming down upon the mountains of Zion; for there the Lord commanded the blessing—life forever* (Psalm 133).

When Joseph, now a great man in Egypt, was first aware that he was facing his brothers, his heart was to know how the rest of his family were doing. He asks questions concerning the welfare of his father and brother (see Gen. 43:7). His brothers tell him that there is still one who stayed behind with their father. Joseph emphatically makes them understand that when they return for more food (blessing), "you shall not see my face unless your brother is with you" (Gen. 43:3b). I believe the greater "Joseph" who has all our provision at His disposal is saying to the Church, "You will not see My face unless your brother(s) are with you." God is a family "man" who longs to see His family united. Jesus expressed this desire so clearly in His high priestly prayer, "I do not ask in behalf of these alone, but for those also who believe in Me through their word; that they may *all* be one; even as Thou Father art in Me and I in Thee" (Jn. 17:20-21a).

I am convinced that God wants to restore unity in the Body of Christ. Keep in mind that there is a difference between unity and conformity. It is not right or healthy for the people of God to be divided. Division is a tool of the devil. "Divide and conquer" is one of satan's primary strategies. It is for these reasons that Paul exhorted the Ephesians to be "diligent to preserve the unity of the Spirit in the bond of peace" (Eph. 4:3).

ZION AND THE RIVER

The river, which has its source in God, gives life. "And he showed me a river of the water of life, clear as crystal, coming from the throne of God and of the Lamb, in the middle of its street. And on either side of the river was the tree of life, bearing twelve kinds of fruit, yielding its fruit every month; and the leaves of the tree were for the healing of the nations" (Rev. 22:1-2). "There is a river whose streams make glad the city of God, the holy dwelling places of the Most High" (Ps. 46:4). This is the purpose of the river: to "make glad" the city of God (Zion) and to bring healing to the nations.

Today we as believers are blessed with a fresh outpouring of God's Spirit on His Church. Like Israel in the wilderness, we have the opportunity to partake of this "spiritual drink" that has come to be called "the river." As thousands of believers can testify—and you may be one of them—the river is a place of spiritual refreshing. However, there is more to the river than just renewal. *With renewal comes responsibility.* God has not poured out the river solely for our blessing and benefit. God has a redemptive purpose behind everything He does. If all we do is simply soak in the river and bask in the blessing, we will miss God's higher purpose for the river. We run the risk of failing to complete the race as Israel did, as well as fail to enter into the fullness of God's purpose for us.

It is important to remember that the river issues from a divine source. The prophet Ezekiel speaks symbolically of a river flowing south from under the eastern threshold of the temple. The water ran past the altar, beginning as a trickle and gradually increasing until it became a great river too deep to ford, making fresh everything it touched (see Ezek. 47:1-8). This river is the source of life. "And it will come about that every living creature which swarms in every place where the river goes, will live. And there will be very many fish, for these waters go there, and the others become fresh; so everything will live where the river goes" (Ezek. 47:9).

Just as the river flowed from within the temple to the outside world, so Jesus said that out of our innermost being would flow rivers of *living* water (see Jn. 7:38). As God no longer dwells in temples made with hands, the river now flows from our bodies, the holy temples of the living God. Many have been deeply refreshed from the current river of God's presence; but we have stopped short of His full purpose to release His river through us that others also may be refreshed.

All believers are citizens of Zion, the city of God. While being "in the river" means refreshing, being "in Zion" means responsibility. Many of us have already been "made glad" by the refreshing of the river. Now it is time to move forward, to work with the Lord to help bring healing to the nations. The river He has poured out to refresh us is also His invitation to join Him in the mission of reconciling the world to Himself. If we let ourselves be satisfied with only the refreshing, we will miss the full purpose of the river.

The river is holy because it comes from God, who is holy. All who enjoy its refreshing are called to a holy life with a holy purpose: to be a holy habitation for the Lord. He wants to be on display in our lives so that others can see Him and come to know Him. In order to prepare ourselves to be habitations of God, though, we must first understand His "culture"—the environment He requires.

ENDNOTES

1. Joe R. Baskin, "Jerusalem," *Holman Bible Dictionary* (Nashville, Tennessee: Holman Bible Publishers, 1991). *Quick Verse 4.0 Deluxe Bible Reference Collection*. CD-ROM. Parsons Technology, 1992-1996.

2. Baskin, "Jerusalem."

3. G.D. Watson, *God's First Words* (Jamestown, North Carolina: Newby Press, n.d.), 114.

Chapter Seven

The Habitation of God

A number of years ago I watched a television documentary on the White House chef. Most of us wouldn't give a second thought to the demands or qualifications of such a job. I was surprised to see just how much is involved. The chef must not only be an expert in the culinary arts with the ability to prepare any type of dish required, bake elaborate cakes and other "goodies," and oversee state dinners for dozens of people, but must also possess cultural sensitivity and a knowledge of varied social customs. It would be a diplomatic disaster, for example, if the prime minister of Israel visited the White House and was treated to a breakfast of ham and eggs, or if a Muslim head of state was offered an alcoholic beverage. Misunderstanding of another's religion, culture, or customs can lead to personal and even national offense. Wars have begun over such things.

When I was 14 years old, my father brought our family from England to America because he was traveling extensively in the United States at that time. For seven years we were based at a Bible school in Minneapolis. I was very quickly shocked to hear swear words coming from the mouths of Christian kids at this school, which was known for its holiness and sanctification. They were equally shocked to hear Leonard Ravenhill's son swearing. I eventually became good friends with these kids, but for a while this swearing caused a bit of a problem. Eventually we realized that we were dealing not with sinful swearing, but with a clash of cultures. Swear words in England are not necessarily swear words in America, and vice versa. Even though we spoke the same language, we represented two different cultures with two different concepts of what constituted swearing.

Cultural offense is not always verbal. In some cultures the familiar American "thumbs up" is an obscene gesture. In others, belching after dinner—considered extremely rude and unmannerly in America—is a sign of one's enjoyment of the meal. Not to belch is to offend one's host.

In Thailand, pointing one's foot at another is considered to be a terrible insult, especially if you show the sole of your foot. To the Thai people the foot is the most despised part of the body. I once heard of an occasion where the entire second floor of a two-story building was evacuated before the king of Thailand entered on the first floor. If they hadn't, the king would have been under their feet, which was unthinkable for someone of his rank and nobility. On another occasion, a man I worked with in New Zealand was at a conference in Thailand, preaching on the subject of David and Goliath. To drive home the part of the story where David slings the stone, this man threw a shoe across the room. When I was in the country a year later, a strong residue of resentment still existed toward this man over what he had done. It was all because he did not understand their culture.

Many years ago my family visited the San Diego Zoo, which is regarded as one of the best zoos in the world. Many of the animals, such as the lions, tigers, elephants, and giraffes, felt quite at home because the climate of southern California is similar to that of Africa. I fear, however, that the polar bear we saw was not quite as comfortable. San Diego is not the best environment for polar bears. The arid heat there is a far cry from the ice and tundra north of the Arctic Circle, which is the bear's natural habitat.

All of this is to say that I believe God has a "natural habitat," a "culture," if you will. His way of doing things is different from ours. Unless we understand that, we can offend Him and end up puzzled as to why our relationship with Him is not everything we would like it to be. We need to understand the habitation of God if we wish to enjoy the fullness of His presence.

A Suitable Dwelling Place

A habitat is the usual place where someone or something is found; it is the environment in which a plant or animal naturally lives and grows. A habitation is a dwelling place, a residence. The English word *habitation* is used to translate several Hebrew words in the Old Testament that have the various meanings of dwelling, house, tabernacle, marry, settle, keep house, rest, and other similar ideas. All these speak of a permanent abode, an established dwelling place. All of us have a habitat, a dwelling place, someplace where we can "hang our hat," relax, rest, and be ourselves.

God too has a dwelling place—Heaven. But He also desires to dwell in the midst of His people. Not long after giving the Ten Commandments on Mount Sinai, the Lord said to Moses, "Let them construct a sanctuary for Me, that I may dwell among them" (Ex. 25:8). Notice that it is God who took the initiative, not Moses. Moses didn't come along trying to twist God's arm, saying, "You know, Lord, it's about time You paid us a visit. After all, we're supposed to be Your kids." God acted in accordance with the desire He has had from the beginning. Like any good father, God wants to be with His family. He wants His children to grow, flourish, and rejoice in His presence.

God told Moses that the Israelites were to build a sanctuary for His dwelling place. The Hebrew word for "sanctuary" is *miqdash*, which means a consecrated or holy place.[1]

It is "a place set aside by men upon God's direction and acceptance as the place where He meets them and they worship Him."[2] God wants to dwell among His people, but a suitable dwelling place must be prepared first.

In this passage in Exodus 25, we find God expressing two things. First, He expresses His desire. Secondly, He expresses His demands. His desire is to dwell among His people; His demands, however, are rigid and exact.

Not just any place will do. Consider the next verse: "According to all that I am going to show you, as the pattern of the tabernacle and the pattern of all its furniture, just so you shall construct it" (Ex. 25:9). God not only desires to abide in the midst of His people, but He also has specific demands regarding the environment and type of dwelling place that is acceptable to Him. He said to Moses, in effect, "I want to be your God and dwell where you dwell, but I won't live just anywhere. I will show you *exactly* what I want in My sanctuary, and *just so you shall construct it.*"

It was not Moses' place to determine what was suitable or acceptable to God in His sanctuary. So God took Moses up on the mountain and showed him the complete plans for the tabernacle—down to every minute detail. The tabernacle (a word that means "dwelling place" or "tent") that the Israelites were to build was patterned after and symbolized the heavenly tabernacle (dwelling place) of God. God said to Moses, "Replicate this pattern on earth exactly in every detail. I want the same habitat on earth that I am used to in Heaven. I want to feel just as at home on earth as I do in Heaven."

During our years in New Zealand, my wife, Nancy, would occasionally purchase a magazine called *Woman's Weekly*. This magazine hardly ever missed having an article featuring something on the British royal family. One day she brought home a copy that caught even my attention. The cover said something about the fact that Prince Charles and Lady Di were to be making a royal visit to Australia and would be staying on a farm. I guess it was the idea of Lady Di spending time on a farm that aroused my curiosity. I had spent some years as a young teen on an Irish farm and could not imagine Lady Di in such an environment. As I hurriedly turned the pages, my fears gave way to full acceptance of the fact that this would be an ideal "home away from home" for them. The article featured photographs of "the farm," and it was a far cry from any farm I had set foot on. It was a magnificent mansion set among gorgeous gardens. The inside shots revealed palace-like rooms, full of the most exquisite and elaborate decor. Everything about the place was fit for a king. I could easily see how the Prince and Princess would have no trouble feeling at home.

You can learn a lot about people simply by visiting their home. As soon as you walk in the door you can tell whether they are rich or poor or in-between. A glance at their bookshelf will give you an idea of their educational level as well as their professional and personal interests: golf, photography, music, art, medicine, law, cooking, etc. Even the furniture is revealing. It may be antique, classic, contemporary, expensive, or cheap—all these say something about the owners.

In chapter 4 of Revelation, John takes us into the house of God, into the heavenly tabernacle, and into the very Holy of Holies itself. This "guided tour" does indeed reveal some very significant truths about God—through where and how He dwells.

WHO'S IN CHARGE HERE?

As we said before, a *habitat* is the place where someone or something is usually found. God's habitat is the throne of Heaven. That is where He is *always* found. There is never a moment when the throne of Heaven is unoccupied. "Throne" in Greek is *thronos*, which means "a seat of authority."[3]

> *After these things I looked, and behold, a door standing open in heaven, and the first voice which I had heard, like the sound of a trumpet speaking with me, said, "Come up here, and I will show you what must take place after these things." Immediately I was in the Spirit; and behold, a throne was standing in heaven, and One sitting on the throne* (Revelation 4:1-2).

"After these things" refers to the messages to the seven churches recorded in chapters 2 and 3. From chapter 1 we know that John was "in the Spirit on the Lord's Day" (verse 10) and that he received visions of "things which must shortly take place" (verse 1). One of these visions is of an open door in Heaven. The Lord invites John to come in. As John crosses the threshold of Heaven, the very first thing he sees is a throne with the Lord sitting on it. Initially, this is all he sees. The authority of that throne and the glory of He who is sitting on it overwhelm John, completely arresting his attention.

So the first thing John sees upon entering Heaven is the Lord sitting on the seat of authority. God is the One who exercises all power in Heaven. His "habitation" is the place of power and authority. Jesus said, "But I say to you, make no oath at all, either by heaven, for it is the throne of God, or by the earth, for it is the footstool of His feet, or by Jerusalem, for it is the city of the great King" (Mt. 5:34-35). These verses speak clearly to God's authority: He sits on the throne, the earth is His footstool (that is, under His authority), and He is the King of the holy city.

God no longer dwells in temples made with hands. At one time there was the tabernacle, then Solomon's Temple, then Zerubbabel's Temple in the days of Ezra and Nehemiah, and finally Herod's Temple, the temple of Jesus' day. Now, however, God dwells, through His Holy Spirit, in the *hearts* of His people. *We* are His temple! Paul said that our bodies are temples of the Holy Spirit (see 1 Cor. 6:19). The Book of Hebrews says, "Now Moses was faithful in all His house as a servant, for a testimony of those things which were to be spoken later; but Christ was faithful as a Son over His house whose house we are, if we hold fast our confidence and the boast of our hope firm until the end" (Heb. 3:5-6).

However, if God is going to reside in your house or in mine, if we are going to experience the fullness of His presence the way we desire, then He demands the throne. It's just that simple. The throne is God's dwelling place. He demands the right to govern, the right to rule, the right to control our lives. When God comes to reside in us, He comes as Lord, Master, and King.

We may ask ourselves, "Why am I not growing spiritually? Why am I so often frustrated with my Christian life? Why don't I have the kind of deep, intimate relationship with God that I want?" It's because we don't understand God's "culture" or His ways. We don't realize that if God's presence is to be fully manifested in us, then He must fully reside on the throne of our lives—without hesitation or equivocation.

I was 18 years old when I surrendered my life to God. For four years I had battled with accepting Christ as my Savior. I knew I was a sinner; that was not the problem. Having been raised in a solid, committed Christian home, I knew what it meant to be a sinner and what it meant to become a Christian. I longed for peace with God, for cleansing, and for the forgiveness of my sins. I wanted to go to Heaven. Perhaps because of my Christian upbringing, however, I knew that God wanted more. My problem was this whole issue of the throne of my life.

At that time, my one goal in life, my supreme desire above all else, was to pursue a profession in the field of graphics. Yet I sensed that if I gave my life to God, He would lead me in a different direction. It was a battle of wills: mine against God's. The struggle went on for four long years. Hundreds of times I literally shook under the conviction of my sin, knowing that God wanted to draw me to Himself, yet I refused to give up the throne.

Finally, at the age of 18, I decided to stop struggling, stop resisting. I said to God, "Here I am, Lord, cleanse me, wash me, forgive me. All that I am is Yours. All that I have I give to You. Here is my life; I surrender it to You. I want You to take over."

If God is going to feel at home in our hearts, if we want a lasting, abiding, and growing relationship with Him, then we must give Him the throne.

HOUSECLEANING

After John's eyes adjust to the splendor of the glory of God around the throne, he begins to see other things in Heaven. Twenty-four thrones surround God's throne with 24 white-robed elders, crowned with gold crowns, sitting on them. Lightning and thunder proceed from the throne; seven firelamps also surround the throne, which were the seven Spirits of God. A sea of crystalline glass shimmers in front of the throne, and four living creatures like a lion, a calf, a man, and an eagle, stand before the throne.

And the four living creatures, each one of them having six wings, are full of eyes around and within; and day and night they do not cease to say, "Holy, holy, holy, is the Lord God, the Almighty, who was and who is and who is to come" (Revelation 4:8).

When the four creatures gave glory and honor to God, the 24 elders fell on their faces and worshiped, saying,

Worthy art Thou, our Lord and our God, to receive glory and honor and power; for Thou didst create all things, and because of Thy will they existed, and were created (Revelation 4:11).

Immediately John becomes aware that God's throne is surrounded by absolute holiness; indeed, it is *thrice* holy. This is why the plan for the tabernacle included a place called the Holy of Holies. That's where God dwelled, in a *most holy place*.

If God is going to dwell in our lives on a permanent basis, if we are to enjoy the full richness of His presence, not only must we give Him the throne, but we also must provide Him with a *holy place*.

Many years ago my wife and I took our children on a farm holiday in New Zealand. Many sheep farmers in New Zealand, when they have a prosperous year, buy up adjacent property for expansion. The new property usually has a house on it. Since the farmer already has a house, he often rents out the other one to people desiring a vacation in the country.

We had heard about a particular house nestled in a beautiful valley, with majestic, snow-capped mountains on either side, and a river running through the middle of it. It sounded absolutely idyllic. I was pastoring at the time and looked forward to getting away for a little while to read, fish, go for walks, and simply relax. Picking up the key, we drove off for our farm holiday, our excitement and anticipation mounting with every mile that we drove through that gorgeous valley.

We arrived at the house, walked inside—and the place was absolutely filthy! The carpet was threadbare, springs poked through the couch cushions, and empty beer and liquor bottles lay all over the kitchen. The condition of the mattress in the bedroom was indescribable. You can imagine our shock and disappointment at discovering that the house was not at all what we had expected. It was obvious that the house had been used as a hunting or fishing lodge where men would come in just to spend the night. They apparently would flop down anywhere on the floor, light a fire, drink or smoke or do whatever else they wanted to do, and simply go out during the day. It was an environment that was completely foreign to us.

Nevertheless, we tried to make the best of it. We finally put enough blankets on the mattress to be able to sleep and told ourselves, "Well, at least in the morning we can get up and go outside." Wouldn't you know it, we woke up the next morning to a torrential rain that lasted for the next four days. For four days we did not leave that house!

Finally, we just couldn't stand it anymore. Packing up our belongings, we cut our "farm holiday" short, explaining to the person we had rented the house from that we were leaving because of the weather. That was only a half-truth, but we didn't want to embarrass her about the condition of the house.

We were so glad to get home! Everything was just the way we liked it: neat, tidy, clean, and comfortable. We felt like saying with Dorothy in *The Wizard of Oz*, "There's no place like home...there's no place like home... there's no place like home!"

There really is no place like home, and God's home is a place of holiness. Yet many of us expect Him to dwell with us when there is uncleanness, rebellion, lust, worldliness, or other unholy things in our lives. Part of the ministry of the Holy Spirit is to point out those things to us and clean them to open up and let Him work. As long as we are cooperating during with those things, everything is fine. It's when we resist that we grieve the Holy Spirit. Persistent resistance will eventually quench the Spirit, and He will withdraw. If we want God to dwell in us, we must present ourselves to Him as clean, pure, and holy vessels.

A.W. Tozer once said that the key to spiritual progress and maturity is to find out what God loves and love it, and to find out what God hates and hate it. When we give God the throne of our lives…when we let the Spirit clean all the filth, dirt, and uncleanness out…when we learn to love what God loves and hate what God hates, then we will begin to understand what it means to create a habitation suitable and acceptable to Him.

Holiness is not simply measured by not doing certain things; it is also measured by the depth of our desire to please the Lord. Too many Christians live their lives out of a sense of duty, not devotion.

When I was in Bible college, I fell in love with a beautiful young lady named Nancy Schultz (now my wife of 34 years). The school we attended was very strict regarding dating. We were permitted off campus only once a month, and, according to the rules, had to be back on campus by 10:30 p.m. Not only were we restricted in this way, but it was enforced by having to "sign in" upon returning to campus. If a person was consistently late, he or she could be expelled from the school. Needless to say, we had great difficulty accepting these rules, which infringed upon our freedom in dating. One day, by "revelation" I chanced upon the idea that there was no rule established as to how early we could leave the campus. Being deeply in love with my girlfriend, I wanted to spend as much time as possible with her. So we would meet as early as 5:00 a.m. and, along with another couple, set off for the day together. By the time 10:30 p.m. arrived, we had no problem complying with the curfew.

There was another rule, however, that I did find difficult to follow, and that was that every student was required to rise early for a personal devotional time before proceeding down to breakfast. This, to me, was a constant battle and one I regretfully confess I failed many times. What was the problem? My relationship with the Lord in those days was not based on devotion, but duty. I had no love relationship; therefore, I struggled to keep the rules. On the other hand, if Nancy had suggested that on our next date we meet at 4:00 a.m., I'm sure I would have jumped out of bed without the slightest hesitation. Why? I was in love!

Far too many Christians try to live by laws rather than love. The Psalmist said, "I delight to do Thy will, O my God" (Ps. 40:8a). Paul said, "We have as our ambition...to be pleasing to Him" (2 Cor. 5:9). What is your delight and ambition? Remember, the river makes everything around it fresh.

AN ATTITUDE OF GRATITUDE

Continuing his look into Heaven, John notices that not only is the throne of God surrounded by an atmosphere of holiness, but also by an atmosphere of thanksgiving. He watches and listens as the four living creatures "give glory and honor and thanks to Him who sits on the throne, to Him who lives forever and ever" (Rev. 4:9). God dwells in the midst of continual thanksgiving. It is a significant part of His habitation.

We need to understand how critical thanksgiving is. Many of us don't think about thanksgiving very often. We remember it once a year on the fourth Thursday of November, for a special emphasis, or after a particularly abundant time of blessing or answered prayer. How many of us, though, make giving thanks a daily *lifestyle*?

Scripture exhorts us over and over to give thanks to God.

O give thanks to the Lord, for He is good; for His lovingkindness is everlasting (1 Chronicles 16:34).

Always giving thanks for all things in the name of our Lord Jesus Christ to God, even the Father (Ephesians 5:20).

In everything give thanks; for this is God's will for you in Christ Jesus (1 Thessalonians 5:18).

It is God's will that we give thanks *in everything*. How faithful are we in obeying this? Giving thanks to God is a healing balm for the spirit. On the other hand, failure to give thanks (ingratitude or indifference) carries consequences. "Because you did not serve the Lord your God with joy and a glad heart, for the abundance of all things; therefore you shall serve your enemies whom the Lord shall send against you" (Deut. 28:47-48a). If that sounds like a rather stiff penalty for ingratitude, it does show the value and importance God places on thanksgiving.

God is surrounded by thanksgiving in Heaven. Giving thanks was a regular part of Jewish worship in the tabernacle, the temple, and in the homes of the faithful. The early Christians learned to live and breathe thankfulness. What about you? Is the voice of constant thanks heard in the temple of *your* heart? If God sniffed the air of your sanctuary, would He smell the sweet, fragrant incense of praise and thanksgiving, or the stench of bitterness, anger, pride, and ingratitude?

In Romans 1, Paul describes the downward spiral of the ungodly into greater and greater sin and depravity (see Rom. 1:18-32). Paul writes, "For even though they knew God, they did not honor Him as God, or give thanks; but they became futile in their speculations, and their foolish heart was darkened" (Rom. 1:21). One of the root causes of their spiritual and moral degradation was ingratitude—lack of thankfulness.

God puts a premium on thanksgiving because, according to Scripture, He inhabits the praises of His people (see Ps. 22:3). Praise and thanksgiving are part of the habitation of God. When we gather together in a spirit of genuine praise, thanksgiving, and worship from pure and sincere hearts, we create an atmosphere that actually draws the presence of God. We also can do it individually when we offer up to God a heart and life that are pure, holy, thankful, and completely surrendered to His Lordship.

Paul and Silas were in jail in Philippi, bound in heavy chains and behind guarded doors. It was dank, dark, and dismal. Around midnight they began praying and singing hymns of praise to God. (How's that for putting a positive "spin" on your situation?) God heard the praise and the prayers and said, "That sounds like home." He came down, the ground shook, the chains fell off, the prison doors opened, and a pagan jailer and his family were brought to Christ—all because of an "attitude of gratitude." God responds powerfully to a thankful heart.

We need to cultivate the sacrifice of thanksgiving in our lives. We take for granted our health, freedom, families, jobs, etc. America is a blessed nation. We are multimillionaires in comparison to what millions of people suffer through on a daily basis in other nations. Not only do we have material and physical blessings, but we also have spiritual blessings that eclipse all else. Make a list of things you are grateful for. Never forget the pit from which you were dug. In the words of the Psalmist, "He brought me up also out of an horrible pit, out of the miry clay, and set my feet upon a rock..." (Ps. 40:2 KJV). Thank You, Lord, for all Your benefits, which You daily load upon us.

The hymnist Thomas Chisholm expressed it so beautifully when he wrote:

> "Great is Thy faithfulness
> Great is Thy faithfulness
> Morning by morning new mercies I see
> All I have needed Thy hand hath provided
> Great is Thy faithfulness, Lord, unto me."[4]

When we talk about offering the sacrifice of thanksgiving or the sacrifice of praise, we should never do so while thinking of it in terms of a sacrifice, which costs something. Imagine the reaction of your wife if, on the day of your wedding anniversary you gave her an expensive gift of jewelry, but then burst into tears and said, "Darling, you can't imagine what this has cost me." The gift may have been expensive, but you don't think of the price you paid; rather, you think of how much you love her and want to make her happy.

To understand the true meaning of "sacrifice," we need to look at the way sacrifices were given in the Old Testament. Every sacrifice was first presented before the priest to be inspected. The priest would examine in detail each sacrifice to make sure it was perfect and without blemish. Only the very best was acceptable to God. With this in mind, when we speak about the sacrifices in the New Testament, we are not thinking in terms of cost, but quality. Our thanksgiving and praise should not be some feeble, halfhearted offering, but rather the very best we can offer. Not all sacrifices were acceptable. That is why the Psalmist prayed, "Let the words of my mouth and the meditation of my heart be acceptable in Thy sight..." (Ps. 19:14). Learn to give God your very best. He is worthy of it.

AND ALL THE PEOPLE SAID, "AMEN!"

In John's vision of Heaven, the throne of God also is filled with an atmosphere of worship. Worship literally means to bow down and kiss the hand of another. It means to place oneself in a lower posture and recognize that He is King. The four living creatures give glory, honor, and thanks to God while the 24 elders fall on their faces before Him, cast their crowns at His feet, and worship Him (see Rev. 4:9-11). A little later, John witnesses the entire created host of Heaven and earth praising and worshiping God:

> ... *"Worthy is the Lamb that was slain to receive power and riches and wisdom and might and honor and glory and blessing."...* *"To Him who sits on the throne, and to the Lamb, be blessing and honor and glory and dominion forever and ever." And the four living creatures kept saying, "Amen." And the elders fell down and worshiped* (Revelation 5:12,13b-14).

The word *amen* is intimately tied with worship in the Bible. It is a powerful word that means to be in agreement with, or to be in harmony with. "Amen" means "So be it!" It is a word not only of absolute agreement, but also of *radical obedience*. In fact, such obedience is at the very heart of true worship.

Genuine worship comes from a heart that is in absolute agreement with God, absolutely committed to God, and resolutely, radically obedient to God. When God told Abraham to offer his son Isaac as a sacrifice, *Abraham did not complain; he complied.* Without question or hesitation Abraham took Isaac to the mountain, placed him on the sacrificial altar, and prepared to slay him—until God stayed his hand and provided a ram to be sacrificed in Isaac's place. That was worship. There was no music, no singing, no preaching, no program—just radical obedience.

When God allowed satan to test Job's faithfulness, Job lost his family, his wealth, and his health. He was reduced to sitting on an ash heap, scraping his sores with a piece of broken pottery. Job didn't understand his suffering and cried out to God. Yet there was an "amen" in his heart. In the midst of his trials he said, "Naked I came from my mother's womb, and naked I shall return there. The Lord gave and the Lord has taken away. Blessed be the name of the Lord" (Job 1:21). Job didn't rail at God, he didn't curse God, he didn't turn away from God. Instead, he worshiped.

When God told David that the child born of his adulterous affair with Bathsheba would die, David secluded himself for a week to seek God and fast and pray for the life of the child. When he was informed that the child was dead, what did David do? Did he get angry at God? Did he lose faith in a God who did not answer his prayers? No. The Bible says that David washed himself, put on clean clothes, and worshiped God (see 2 Sam. 12:20). David had an "amen" spirit. Despite his pain and sorrow he accepted God's will as right and just. That's worship. No wonder the Bible says that David was a man after God's own heart (see Acts 13:22).

True worship is that response to the will of God in which, no matter how difficult or radical a thing He asks you to do, there is no objection, no resistance, only an "amen" in your spirit that says, "I agree with You, Lord." It is a trusting acceptance that God's will is right, His justice fair, and His purpose perfect. "Amen" worship is a radical abandonment of ourselves to the will and purpose of God.

Jesus said to the Samaritan woman, "But an hour is coming, and now is, when the true worshipers shall worship the Father in spirit and truth; for such people the Father seeks to be His worshipers. God is spirit, and those who worship Him must worship in spirit and truth" (Jn. 4:23-24). No wonder the Father seeks those who will worship Him, because true worship is a rare commodity. Too often we become so preoccupied, so need-conscious, so self-conscious, that we cannot worship because we are focused on ourselves.

God is looking for those who will abandon themselves completely to Him, casting everything at His feet. These are the ones who take their crowns—all their achievement, their prestige, their recognition, and their rewards—cast them down, and worship Him. These are the ones in whom God will choose to dwell in His fullness.

If we're going to grow into the things of God, into the fullness of His presence with the strength and stability to finish the race, we must come to the place of absolute surrender to God's will and ways. We must say to Him with a sincere and pure heart,

*Lord, take the throne of my life. I give it to You. Make me into a holy habitation acceptable to You. Clean out the worldliness that has so controlled my life—the lust, the pride, the bitterness, the resentment, the uncleanness. Take it all out. I want to be a clean vessel, a holy habitation for Your presence and glory. Teach me to be grateful. Let thanksgiving rise up new every morning, like Your mercies, for great is Your faithfulness. Teach me how to worship You in spirit and in truth. Give me an "amen" in my heart of absolute surrender and radical obedience. Amen, **so be it**!*

ENDNOTES

1. James Strong, *Strong's Exhaustive Concordance of the Bible* (Peabody, Massachusetts: Hendrickson Publishers, n.d.), **miqdash**, (#H4720).

2. W.E. Vine, Merrill F. Unger, and William White, Jr., *Vine's Complete Expository Dictionary of Old and New Testament Words* (Nashville, Tennessee: Thomas Nelson Publishers, 1985), to sanctify (**miqdas**), Old Testament section, 213.

3. Vine, Unger, and White, *Vine's Complete Expository Dictionary*, throne (**thronos**), New Testament section, 631.

4. Thomas Obediah Chisholm, "Great Is Thy Faithfulness," © 1923. Renewal 1951 by Hope Publishing Co., Carol Stream, Illinois. All rights reserved. Used by permission.

Chapter Eight

Worship: The Rare Jewel

THE knock on the door was to change our lives forever. The year was 1951. I was nine years old and living in England with my mother and two brothers. My father, Leonard Ravenhill, was in the U.S. on an extended ministry trip. He had retired for the night after speaking for A.W. Tozer at the Alliance Church in Chicago. All was peaceful as he slept soundly in his third-floor room at a local Chicago hotel where he was suddenly awakened by the fire alarm. The knock on the door told us the rest of the story.

Unable to make his way down the stairs due to the fire and smoke, my father was forced to return to his room. His Irish prayer partner and traveling companion, Tom Hare, by this time was incapacitated. My father had no option but to drop his friend out of the window and then proceed to jump himself.

During those few fleeting seconds as he was falling, the Spirit of God spoke to him from Psalm 118:17 (KJV): "[Thou] shall not die, but live, and declare the works of the Lord." Seconds later, he lay in agony, his back and legs broken by the fall.

Now the police were informing my mother that the hospital said he would not live through the night. Within an hour, plans were made for my mother to fly to the States. I was taken to a neighbor who attended our church. My two brothers went to another church family.

Miraculously, my father lived. As he lay in the hospital totally immobilized, his body and legs in plaster, he said to the Lord, "Now what good am I? I can't preach anymore. I can't even read my Bible." As he lay there, he heard the gentle but firm voice of God say, "You can worship Me."

After 30 years of ministry, I am convinced that worship is one of the most neglected teachings in the Word of God. It is one of the most misunderstood and therefore least-practiced elements of Christian and church life. Because we have not understood what it means to worship, both we as individual believers and the Church as a whole are impoverished. We are like dirt-poor farmers scratching out a bare subsistence from the land while, unknown to us, acres of diamonds lie just inches below the surface.

THE PRIORITY OF WORSHIP

True worship is the rarest of jewels in the Church today. It is a calling that surpasses that of the apostle, the prophet, the evangelist, the pastor, the teacher, or any other ministry. The call to worship is extended to every believer, young or old, mature or immature. God expects and commands His people to worship. One of the serious problems in the Church today is that, although worship is demanded of every Christian, it is experienced by very few. In most of our churches, the majority of believers have rarely, if ever, entered into an encounter with God in genuine worship.

Concerning worship, A.W. Tozer wrote,

> "We are called to an everlasting preoccupation with God....Man was made to worship God. God gave to man a harp and said, 'Here above all the creatures that I have made and created I have given you the largest harp...you can worship Me in a manner that no other creature can.' And when he sinned man took that instrument and threw it down in the mud....We're here to be worshippers first and workers only second. We take a convert and immediately make a worker out of him. God never meant it to be so. God meant that a convert should learn to be a worshipper, and after that he can learn to be a worker. The work done by a worshipper will have eternity in it."[1]

On the same subject, A.P. Gibbs made this statement: "That quality of worship which does not result in service, and that service which does not flow from worship, both come short of the Divine ideal."[2]

T. Austin Sparks said,

> "The beginning of every thing in relationship to God is worship; that is, God having the central and supreme place of recognition, of acknowledgment, of government...God having supreme right in our complete obedience and surrender—in every part and phase of our being. Worship begins there. It is a relationship, not only an exercise. It is not something that we do in specified ways

and methods; it is an attitude of the life—a place that God has in the entire consciousness…that is worship."[3]

Most of us regard praise music and worship as synonymous. This is a misconception. Music is certainly an important part of worship, but true worship encompasses far more than just music. In fact, some of the most significant acts of worship in the Scriptures have no music associated with them at all. Worship is the unreserved giving of everything we have to God in recognition of who He is and of His worth; it is acknowledging God's "worth-ship." The three quotes above make it clear that worship is not a ritual or exercise but an attitude of life, where God has absolute first place in the thoughts, affections, and consciousness of a person.

God places the highest priority on worship.

You shall worship the Lord your God and serve Him only (Luke 4:8b).

But an hour is coming, and now is, when the true worshipers shall worship the Father in spirit and truth; for such people the Father seeks to be His worshipers (John 4:23).

Everything in our Christian lives is to flow from worship. The quality of our service and discipleship depends on the quality of our worship. Church, we need to wake up! That which God deems to be the most important is what we relegate the least amount of time to doing. God actively seeks true worshipers; a true worshiper is a rare commodity. What priority does worship have in *your* life? Can you drink from the river and not worship Him?

Who Do We Worship?

One problem with our worship in so many of our churches today is that we tend to eclipse the *object* of worship with *how* we worship. We get caught up in the music, the singing, the dancing, the waving of banners, or whatever, and lose sight of God.

The influence of the erotic spirit is felt almost everywhere in evangelical circles. Much of the singing in certain types of meetings has in it more of romance than it has of the Holy Ghost. Both words and music are designed to rouse the libidinous. Christ is courted with a familiarity that reveals a total ignorance of who He is. It is not the reverent intimacy of the adoring saint but the impudent familiarity of the carnal lover.[4]

Too often we seek an emotion-centered *experience* rather than a reality-based encounter with the One who is the way, the truth, and the life. We focus on manifestations of the Spirit instead of seeking to know Him whose Spirit indwells us. Visually oriented as we are, we easily substitute symbolism for substance.

Growing up with movies and television has made us very entertainment-oriented. This desire to be entertained has influenced our concept and understanding of worship. For many Christians, "worship" is more a program or performance to watch than it is a divine encounter in which they can personally participate. If the service makes them feel good, if the music sends a thrill up their spine, or if the preaching stirs their emotions, then they feel that certainly they must have worshiped, even if they had no conscious awareness of the presence of God.

That kind of "worship" is like going to a birthday party where you get caught up in admiring the decorations, enjoying the cake and ice cream, and playing the games, only to realize on your way home that you never even spoke to the guest of honor. It was his birthday and his party, and you were there, but you ignored him.

Genuine worship focuses on one Person and one Person only. As Father, Son, and Holy Spirit, God alone is worthy of our worship. He is the One who created the heavens and the earth, the moon and the stars, and holds them in their places. He is the One who raises up and brings down kingdoms. He is the One Isaiah saw "sitting on a throne, lofty and exalted, with the train of His robe filling the temple. Seraphim stood above Him...And one called out to another and said, 'Holy, Holy, Holy, is the Lord of hosts, the whole earth is full of His glory' " (Is. 6:1b-3).

We must be careful always to keep the focus of our worship squarely on God Himself. It is too easy for us to fall into the trap of worshiping our own worship. It is too easy to lift up human talent, ability, or understanding to the point that we take away from God the honor that is due His name. Everything we do in worship should go first to the cross of Christ. Much of our worship ignores the cross because we actually are lifting up man.

Allowing the *means* of worship to eclipse the *object* of worship is a form of idolatry, and God warns us against it time after time in His Word. False worship was one of the indictments against Israel. "Then the Lord said, 'Because this people draw near with their words and honor Me with their lip service, but they remove their hearts far from Me, and their reverence for Me consists of tradition learned by rote' " (Is. 29:13). The Israelites went through the ritual of worship, but there was no heart in it.

We need to examine our motives and our desires. Why are we worshiping? Is it because we want to bring glory to God and grow in intimate fellowship with Him? Or is it because we want to be entertained and made to feel good? We need to regularly ask, "Lord, is this taking away from Your glory?"

WHY WORSHIP?

King Solomon wrote in Ecclesiastes, "All the rivers flow into the sea, yet the sea is not full. To the place where the rivers flow, there they flow again" (Eccles. 1:7). He is talking about the recurring cycle of precipitation and evaporation. Rain falls to the earth, the earth siphons it to the rivers, and the rivers run to the sea. Yet the sea is never full because evaporation occurs, the water returns to the heavens from whence it came, and the cycle begins again.

That is a picture of worship: giving back to God what is due Him and that came from Him. Charles Spurgeon once said that worship "is the work of the Spirit in the soul returning to its author." Worship is our response to God's love, grace, mercy, kindness, and goodness. To know God is to worship Him.

Paul put it this way to the Romans:

For who has known the mind of the Lord, or who became His counselor? Or who has first given to Him that it might be paid back to him again? For from Him and through Him and to Him are all things. To Him be the glory forever. Amen. I urge you therefore, brethren, by the mercies of God, to present your bodies a living and holy sacrifice, acceptable to God, which is your spiritual service of worship (Romans 11:34–12:1).

Everything we have and everything we are we have received from God. Anything we ever receive or become will be from Him. It is in Him that we live, move, and have our being. He is the One to whom we owe all things. Simply stated, worship is the unreserved giving of everything back to God. Even more, it is the unreserved giving of ourselves to God in absolute love and devotion. We give ourselves to God in worship because, in Christ, He gave Himself for us. We love Him because He first loved us.

WHAT IS WORSHIP?

The word *worship* first occurs in chapter 22 of Genesis in connection with Abraham's offering his son Isaac to the Lord. After traveling three days to the mountain that God had indicated, Abraham said to the men attending him, "I and the lad will go yonder; and we will *worship* and return to you" (Gen. 22:5b). Abraham was acting in obedience to God's command. On the mountain he built an altar, spread the wood on it, bound his son Isaac, and laid him on the altar. Abraham was about to slay his son when the Lord stopped him, providing a ram to sacrifice instead of Isaac.

With that event, Abraham passed the test. God knew that He had Abraham's heart. "Now I know that you fear God, since you have not withheld your son, your only son, from Me" (Gen. 22:12b). Then God reaffirmed His covenant with Abraham and His promise to make of Abraham a great nation through whom all the earth would be blessed, "because you have obeyed My voice" (Gen. 22:18b).

There is an old but valid principle for interpreting Scripture that we don't hear much about anymore. It is called "the law of first mention." According to this principle, how a word or concept is used the first time it appears in the Bible sets a precedent for how that word or concept is to be understood throughout the rest of the Scriptures.

Abraham worshiped on the mountain. By the law of first mention, Abraham's act of worship established a precedent for understanding worship throughout the Bible. What characterized Abraham's worship on this occasion? Abraham offered up to God his absolute surrender, unquestioning obedience, and unwavering trust. What a precedent!

God was after something in Abraham's life: his heart. God is always after people's hearts because, if He has our heart, he has *us*. "For the eyes of the Lord move to and fro throughout the earth that He may strongly support those whose heart is completely His" (2 Chron. 16:9a).

What does the Bible mean when it speaks of the heart of man? Following the principle of the law of first mention, the first three appearances of the word *heart* in the Bible are revealing. The first two occurrences are in successive verses in Genesis 6; the third appears two chapters later.

> *Then the Lord saw that the wickedness of man was great on the earth, and that every intent of the thoughts of his heart was only evil continually. And the Lord was sorry that He had made man on the earth, and He was grieved in His heart* (Genesis 6:5-6).

> *And the Lord smelled the soothing aroma; and the Lord said to Himself, "I will never again curse the ground on account of man, for the intent of man's heart is evil from his youth; and I will never again destroy every living thing, as I have done"* (Genesis 8:21).

"The thoughts of his heart" refers to the mind; "grieved in His heart" involves the emotions; and "the intent of [the] heart" points to the will. When God says that He wants our heart, it means that He is after our mind, our emotions, and our will. He wants us to come to the place of total yieldedness to Himself in those three areas, so that He might have complete control over our thinking, our feeling, and our doing. That's what true worship is all about. God is looking for people who will worship Him from their heart.

God tested Abraham at the point of his greatest earthly love: Isaac. Abraham demonstrated by his obedience that his love for God was greater than his love for anything or anyone else, even his precious and long-awaited son. Abraham's heart was undivided; he belonged to God mind, emotions, and will.

God tests us the same way. He always targets the area of our greatest love, asking, "Do I truly have your heart?" He searches for an undivided heart, asking as Jesus did of Peter, "Do you love Me more than these?" (Jn. 21:15b) True worshipers have no unsurrendered areas of their lives. Their heart belongs completely to God. Oh, would to God that we had this kind of worship in our churches, where everything is laid on the altar and where we hold *nothing* back! The object of our love is the object of our worship. We must surrender *everything* to God so that He can become our everything.

Hymn writer Judson W. Van DeVenter expressed it beautifully with these words:

> "All to Jesus I surrender;
> All to Him I freely give.
> I will ever love and trust Him;
> In His presence daily live.
> I surrender all,
> I surrender all.
> All to Thee, my blessed Savior,
> I surrender all."[5]

THE PRICE OF WORSHIP

Genuine worship requires everything of us. Abraham was required to give up his son Isaac. The fact that Isaac did not have to actually die on that altar is irrelevant. Before God stayed his hand, as far as Abraham was concerned, Isaac was already dead. God had commanded the sacrifice and Abraham was committed to obey. However, Abraham knew something about God that everyone learns who abandons himself to Him: God is faithful. If we never learn to trust God, we will never learn how faithful He is. The writer of the Book of Hebrews spoke of Abraham's faith:

> *By faith Abraham, when he was tested, offered up Isaac; and he who had received the promises was offering up his only begotten son;...He considered that God is able to raise men even from the*

dead; from which he also received him back as a type (Hebrews 11:17,19).

Abraham knew that God was faithful and true to His Word. God had promised Abraham a nation of descendants through Isaac, and Abraham knew that God would fulfill that promise even if it meant bringing Isaac back from the dead. Abraham did not focus as much on the sacrifice required as he did on the promise to be fulfilled. This is one of the secrets of genuine worship. True worshipers never think in terms of what they have to give up; rather, they think of what they gain.

God seeks worshipers who hold no treasure so dear that they are not willing to release it to Him. Their love for Him surpasses that of all others: love of family, friends, country, ministry, reputation, whatever. The Father is looking for those who will say, "Lord, there is no sacrifice that I am not prepared to give."

One of the greatest and yet most controversial love stories of all time was surely that of King Edward VIII, who took over the British throne following the death of his father King George V in 1936.

King Edward, formerly the Prince of Wales, was an avid traveler and was called by many "The Empire's Salesman." He was a man whose charm and spirit made him immensely popular with the people. Following his coronation as king, he was known to show great compassion for the welfare of his people, especially those considered to be underprivileged and of the working class.

Before becoming king, Edward had met and fallen in love with a twice-divorced American woman. His romance with Mrs. Simpson soon shook the British empire and rocked the Church of England. As king, he faced the decision of his life: either to remain as King of England and preside over the affairs of the vast British empire or to abdicate the throne for the woman he loved.

In his now famous radio broadcast to the empire, he made what one has described as the greatest declaration of love in history. "I have found it impossible to carry the heavy burden of responsibility and to discharge my duties as king as I would wish to do without the help and support of the woman I love." With these words, he gave up his throne and later married. His love meant more to him than title, position, wealth, or fame. He gladly gave up everything for the one he loved.

Extravagant love validates an extravagant sacrifice. In chapter 14 of Mark's Gospel, a woman comes to Jesus with an alabaster bottle filled with very expensive perfume, breaks open the bottle, and pours it all on Jesus' head. Immediately the woman encounters harsh criticism from some of those present. "Why has this perfume been wasted? For this perfume might have been sold for over three hundred denarii, and the money given to the poor" (Mk. 14:4b-5a). Three hundred denarii was the equivalent of a year's wages. Jesus, however, praised the woman for her faith and defended her unrestrained expression of love. "But Jesus said, 'Let her alone; why do you bother her? She has done a good deed to Me....And truly I say to you, wherever the gospel is preached in the whole world, that also which this woman has done shall be spoken of in memory of her' " (Mk. 14:6,9).

This woman did not count the cost or consider the extravagance of her gift. Instead, she focused on what she gained: the forgiveness of her sins. She was in love and expressed it in the most unmistakable way she could. Her sacrifice was in proportion to the depth of her love. In Luke's account of the same event Jesus says, "Her sins, which are many, have been forgiven, for she loved much; but he who is forgiven little, loves little" (Lk. 7:47b). God honors extravagant sacrifices that are expressions of pure love. When was the last time you took a year's salary and "wasted" it on the Lord?

WORSHIP'S POSITION

I and the lad will go yonder; and we will worship and return to you (Genesis 22:5b).

Come, let us worship and bow down; let us kneel before the Lord our Maker (Psalm 95:6).

The basic Hebrew word for worship is *shachah*, which means to prostrate, bow down, crouch, fall down, fall flat, humbly beseech, do obeisance, do reverence, and make to stoop.[6] Clearly, the idea conveyed by this word is one of abject humility in the presence of a superior. The 24 elders that John saw around God's throne in Revelation 4 worshiped God by falling on their faces. Such a posture in worship is found throughout Scripture.

Matthew's Gospel records the visit of the magi to the young child Jesus, along with their beautiful act of worship. "And they came into the house and saw the Child with Mary His mother; and they fell down and worshiped Him; and opening their treasures they presented to Him gifts of gold and frankincense and myrrh" (Mt. 2:11). These men had sacrificed a lot to find Jesus. When they found Him, they gave extravagant gifts and fell on their faces and worshiped Him. They gave the very best they had and humbled themselves before Him.

Bowing, kneeling, stooping, lying prostrate—all are gestures of respect to one who is superior in person, position, and power. These are positions of surrender, submission, and servitude.

One time, years ago when I was teaching in Korea, I was walking down some stairs to teach a class. A number of young Korean women were coming up the stairs. As they passed me, each of them bent low. It was their custom to so acknowledge a teacher, someone who was higher than themselves in position or authority. It was an expression of great respect.

On the little South Pacific islands of Tonga it is customary for those who address elders to put themselves in a position lower than that of the elder as acknowledgment of his higher position of authority, power, and respect.

Our physical posture in worship is not as important as the posture of our heart. God is not looking just for the bending of our physical frame; He is seeking a humble spirit that is willing to bow down. It is one thing to bow our knee; it is quite another to bow our will, our emotions, and our mind and say, "God, I take a lesser place. You are great, You are mighty, You are holy, and I yield to You. I surrender myself to You unreservedly."

THE PURITY OF WORSHIP

One day while resting at a well, Jesus engaged a Samaritan woman in conversation. They spoke of many things. When the woman perceived that Jesus was a prophet who apparently knew the intimate details of her personal life—perhaps in an attempt to shift the focus away from her moral failures—the woman brought up the subject of worship.

The woman said to Him, "Sir, I perceive that You are a prophet. Our fathers worshiped in this mountain, and you people say that in Jerusalem is the place where men ought to worship." Jesus said to her, "Woman, believe Me, an hour is coming when neither in this mountain, nor in Jerusalem, shall you worship the Father. You worship that which you do not know; we worship that which we know, for salvation is from the Jews. But an hour is coming, and now is, when the true worshipers shall worship the Father in spirit and truth; for such people the Father seeks to be His worshipers. God is spirit, and those who worship Him must worship in spirit and truth" (John 4:19-24).

When Jesus spoke of worshiping "in spirit and truth," He was talking about internal qualities. The woman's concept of worship centered on external things, such as the proper geographical location, a specific place or building, the correct rites and rituals, and so forth. She was spiritually mind-ed in a superficial sort of way. Perhaps it is more accurate to say that she was "religious" but not spiritual. She knew about God but did not know God. Caught up in externals, this woman had never given her heart to God.

Jesus helped her understand that while man looks at the outward appearance, God looks at the heart. Nothing is hidden from God. He knows everything about us, both the good and the bad. How often had this woman participated in "worship" while concealing the moral and spiritual corrup-tion that was in her heart? Such dishonesty before God is sin. Such dishon-esty before men is hypocrisy.

How often have we come into "worship" weighed down by burden-some moral, emotional, or spiritual baggage? How often do we cling to guilt and shame with a death-grip because we are afraid someone else will find out or because we don't really believe that God can or will take it away? It's easy to honor God with our lips and yet have our hearts far away from Him. It happens all the time.

God is looking for purity in our worship; He's looking for honesty, sin-cerity, and humility. That's what it means to worship in spirit and truth. Lis-ten to what the psalmist David said: "Behold, Thou dost desire truth in the innermost being, and in the hidden part Thou wilt make me know wisdom" (Ps. 51:6). "Who may ascend into the hill of the Lord? And who may stand in His holy place? He who has clean hands and a pure heart, who has not lifted up his soul to falsehood, and has not sworn deceitfully" (Ps. 24:3-4). The apostle Paul wrote, "For we are the true circumcision, who worship in the Spirit of God and glory in Christ Jesus and put no confidence in the flesh" (Phil. 3:3).

THE POWER OF WORSHIP

True worshipers are God-centered, not self-centered. Remember, as A.W. Tozer said, worshipers have an "everlasting preoccupation with God." That is the secret to powerful worship. When we enter into true worship, we lose sight of ourselves in the brilliance of God's glory and presence. Our attention is drawn toward Heaven and away from earth.

On the occasions when my father was in Chicago, he had an open invi-tation to visit A.W. Tozer. On one such visit my father knocked on Tozer's door around one or two o'clock in the afternoon. Tozer rose from the small, threadbare mat he used for his private prayer time, invited my father in, and they began to talk. Tozer said that he had arrived in the office that morning around 8:30 or 9:00 with so much to do that he knew he would never get it done unless he spent some time in prayer before the Lord. Then he said to my father, "When you knocked on my door, I hadn't even begun to pray yet; all I've done is worship." That's preoccupation with God!

Why do we get so confused about worship? Why do we have so many struggles in our Christian lives? Why is there so much about God that we don't understand? Certainly, God is beyond the full understanding of our finite capabilities. Nevertheless, we understand so little about Him because we spend so little time in His presence. We are confused about worship because we do not take the time to learn or to let Him teach us. We struggle in our Christian lives, at least in part, because our hearts are not fully surrendered to the Lord.

I believe that God's power is released through true worshipers, those yielded people who do not withhold anything. Abraham did not withhold even Isaac, and God blessed him. God released His power through Abraham and eventually the whole world was blessed because of his faithfulness.

Do you have an "Isaac" that you are struggling to release to the Lord? It may be finances, reputation, ministry, a girlfriend or a boyfriend, or some other thing. Is there anything you are holding onto, that you are not allowing God to have? What God wants us to hear is this:

"When I know I have your heart, I'll give you everything."

I'm convinced that God is looking for "Abrahams" who have totally surrendered their "Isaacs" to Him without any reservations or conditions. When God sees their desire to be wholly His, He reciprocates by giving them His all. With Abraham, God said, "Because you have done this thing, and have not withheld your son, your only son, indeed I will greatly bless you…" (Gen. 22:16b-17).

Many times the measure of God's blessing toward us is restricted by our unwillingness to give everything unreservedly to Him. When we withhold something from God, we are in essence saying, "I love this 'thing' more than I love You." But when we do come to the place of giving everything, God's response is to not withhold anything from us.

May God grant us a revelation of this principle—we have yet to see what God can do through a people whose only desire is to please Him. When we learn to worship in spirit and truth—in honesty, sincerity, and humility—God's power will be released in us and we will enter into the fullness of His plan and purpose. Not only will we be blessed, but we also will be a blessing as God uses us to reach all the peoples of the world with the good news of Jesus Christ. We will have fulfilled God's purpose; we will have drunk from the river and *crossed* the wilderness!

ENDNOTES

1. A.W. Tozer, quoted in Extracts from the *Writings of A.W. Tozer* (Weston-super-Mare, England: Send the Light Trust, 1969), 5-7.

2. A.P. Gibbs, *Worship: The Christian's Highest Occupation* (Kansas City, Kansas: Walterick Publishers, n.d.), 12.

3. T. Austin Sparks, *Living Water from Deep Wells of Revelation* (Corinna, Maine: Three Brothers, n.d.), 132.

4. James Snyder, comp. *Tozer on Worship and Entertainment*, (Camp Hill, Christian Publications, 1997), 76.

5. Public domain.

6. James Strong, *Strong's Exhaustive Concordance of the Bible* (Peabody, Massachusetts: Hendrickson Publishers, n.d.), **shachah**, (#H7812).

Chapter Nine

From Privilege to Purpose

LIKE Israel of old, we in the Church are children of great privilege. God is pouring out a river again, and we are privileged to be a part of it. But He is touching and refreshing us, blessing and enriching our lives for a *purpose*—and He wants us to join Him in accomplishing that purpose.

God is restoring life to the Church. He is rekindling our passion for Him. He is renewing our desire to be faithful and fruitful; the river is flowing once again. In the past we became weary in well doing, but now He is reviving us and restoring our energy. It feels good, and we are really enjoying ourselves. The danger, however, is that we become enamored with playing in the river and never go any farther.

Jesus said, "If any man is thirsty, let him come to Me and drink. He who believes in Me, as the Scripture said, 'From his innermost being shall flow rivers of living water' " (Jn. 7:37b-38). The next verse identifies the "living water" as the Holy Spirit. I see two things here. First, there is the *privilege* of quenching our thirst ("come to Me and drink") and second, there is the *purpose* of allowing ourselves to be channels through whom the life-giving "water" of the Spirit flows out to the world. The first is easy; the second requires commitment, discipline, and sacrifice. You see, God wants us to be like artesian springs, where water bubbles up spontaneously from deep within and floods out over the land.

In these heady days of the "river" we must be careful to keep a clear focus. Too often we chase an experience rather than a relationship. Like children, we run from river to river, always seeking another drink or another place to play. However, at some point we need to stop and sink our own well.

We need to learn that privilege brings responsibility and that true spiritual fulfillment is found not in hiking back and forth between the rivers of experience but in camping at the well of relationship. True satisfaction comes not from the blessings of the Lord but from knowing Him and loving Him.

As we get to know the Lord, we will come to understand His purpose. As we grow to love Him, we will set our hearts and minds to pursue His purpose. That's the kind of people God is looking for. He is seeking those who will drink from the river but never lose sight of the goal, who understand that the refreshing of the river leads naturally to the discipline of the race.

TESTED AT THE RIVER

It was a time of unrest and uncertainty. The Midianites were raiding the land regularly, stealing the Jews' grain and other crops. Gideon was threshing wheat in his father's winepress to hide it from the Midianites when God spoke to him: "The Lord is with you, O valiant warrior....Go in this your strength and deliver Israel from the hand of Midian. Have I not sent you?...Surely I will be with you, and you shall defeat Midian as one man" (Judg. 6:12,14,16).

Gideon sent messengers throughout the land calling men to follow him. Before long a host of 32,000 had gathered. The Lord told Gideon that there were too many; otherwise the people could boast of defeating Midian in their own strength. When Gideon said that any who were fearful could return home, 22,000 left. But God said the 10,000 who remained were still too many.

> *Then the Lord said to Gideon, "The people are still too many; bring them down to the water and I will test them for you there."...So he brought the people down to the water. And the Lord said to Gideon, "You shall separate everyone who laps the water with his tongue, as a dog laps, as well as everyone who kneels to drink." Now the number of those who lapped, putting their hand to their mouth, was 300 men; but all the rest of the people kneeled to drink water. And the Lord said to Gideon, "I will deliver you with the 300 men who lapped and will give the Midianites into your hands; so let all the other people go, each man to his home"* (Judges 7:4a,5-7).

The water became a testing ground for Gideon's men, to see whether they knelt to drink selfishly and with abandon, or whether they carefully lapped it up from their hands in order to keep their eyes on the purpose at hand—which was watching out for the Midianites. The first group (9,700) was focused more on their own needs and comforts than they were on their mission. Gazing into the clear water they no doubt became enamored with their own "image" reflected there. How readily we become mesmerized with "self." This preoccupation with ourselves has caused thousands to miss their calling and purpose. The second group (300) kept the objective clearly in mind; for the moment, their personal needs or desires were secondary. God told Gideon, "These 300 are the men I will use."

I am convinced that, in the same way, God is testing the Church today to see whether we will drink selfishly from the river or whether we will keep our eyes on our objective. He wants to know, "Why are you drinking from the river? Are 'spiritual goose bumps' all you are after, or do you have a higher motivation?" Those who drink from the river solely for the "rush" it gives will eventually find that it no longer satisfies, because it is not designed to apart from God's higher purpose. God will use—and bless—those who are alert to what He is wanting to do and who yield themselves to Him to do it.

FROM CONVERSION TO CALLING

One problem of the Church today is that we concentrate so much on conversion and talk so little about calling. We work hard to get people saved, then do very little to help them learn how to pursue their purpose in God. We are so concerned about getting people *into* the Kingdom of God that we never teach them how to live effectively as citizens *of* the Kingdom of God.

Now, don't get me wrong. Conversion is critical. After all, it's the starting point for fulfilling God's purpose. The problem, however, is that for many Christians, where they start is also where they stop. Crossing the starting line, they never complete their race. They spend the rest of their lives standing just across the line, never venturing far enough to become participants. Ever remaining babes in Christ, they never mature beyond milk to the solid meat of God's Word. Such believers make themselves useless for God's purpose. Remember that you can have a saved soul but a lost life, and that is not God's purpose for any of us.

Another problem in the Church today is that we tend to get so engrossed in the *subject* of Christianity that we lose sight of its *object*— which is to fulfill God's purpose in taking Christ to the nations. Many of us seem satisfied to know a lot about God rather than desire to develop a deep, personal, and intimate relationship with Him. Content with a mental knowledge of Scripture, we are careful not to let God's Word get close enough to us to make a difference in our lives, our habits, and our attitudes. We are more interested in *knowing* than we are in *being*. It's rather like a medical student who studies hard and becomes an expert in every branch of medicine, but who never practices. He is so focused on *learning* how to heal people that he never gets around to *doing* it.

If we're not careful, we can fall easily into the trap of substituting knowledge for relationship. We can become so busy training and learning and preparing that we never get around to doing God's purpose. We run to this conference or that seminar; we enroll in this Bible school or that workshop. Please don't misunderstand; there's nothing wrong with knowledge. Preparation and training are good, useful, and usually a necessary part of pursuing God's purpose effectively. My point is that we must make sure God is leading us in each of these areas.

There comes a time when we must move forward and put what we have learned into action. No time of preparation is complete, no training period finished, until the knowledge learned has been applied to real life. God's purpose is not academic; we can't fulfill it by staying in the classroom or laboratory. God's purpose is worked out through patient, faithful labor and obedience to God in the crucible of everyday experience.

Pursuing God's Purpose

God's purpose never changes, but each generation of believers must seek out and discern God's means and methods for serving His purpose in their generation. This has been true throughout history. Pursuing God's purpose means being committed to hear His voice, obey His commands, and follow His will—even when we do not completely understand. The Bible is full of examples of people who followed God this way and were faithful to His purpose in their generation.

> *By faith Abraham, when he was called, obeyed by going out to a place which he was to receive for an inheritance; and he went out, not knowing where he was going. By faith he lived as an alien in the land of promise, as in a foreign land, dwelling in tents with Isaac and Jacob, fellow heirs of the same promise; for he was looking for the city which has foundations, whose architect and builder is God* (Hebrews 11:8-10).

Abraham left his homeland knowing only that God had called him and was leading him forward. He trusted God to take care of everything else. Because of his faithfulness, God blessed Abraham and made a great nation of him. Abraham fulfilled God's purpose in his generation.

For David, after he had served the purpose of God in his own generation, fell asleep, and was laid among his fathers... (Acts 13:36).

David understood God's purpose as well as his own role and calling in fulfilling that purpose for his particular generation and time. As a man after God's own heart, David devoted his life to serving the Lord and his heart and energy to pursuing His purpose. Each of us should be able to substitute our names for David's in this verse. May the testimony of our lives be that we served the purpose of God in our own generation!

For I did not shrink from declaring to you the whole purpose of God (Acts 20:27).

Paul was addressing the elders of the church in Ephesus before saying good-bye to them for the last time. He understood God's purpose and was absolutely and totally committed to pursuing that purpose in his generation. His testimony at the end of his life was that he had declared the whole purpose of God; he had finished the course and kept the faith. As a result, through Paul's efforts and faithfulness, the gospel spread to every region of the Roman empire.

Many others were just as faithful as Paul. Although their names and stories have not come down to us, because of their faithfulness, they were used of God in their generation to accomplish His purpose. God always uses those who are willing to trust and follow Him without having to know everything up front.

Likewise, God has a purpose, a *calling*, for each and every one of us. As believers we are called to pursue the purpose of God in our generation. Conversion and calling are inseparable. To be saved is to be called; it's automatic. Paul wrote to Timothy, "[God] has saved us, and called us with a holy calling, not according to our works, but according to His own purpose and grace which was granted us in Christ Jesus from all eternity" (2 Tim. 1:9).

God has saved us *and* called us *according to His own purpose*. We cannot serve God's purpose in a past generation, nor can we do so for a future generation (except in the training and preparation we give our children). The only generation we can serve is our own, and that is the only one God holds us responsible for.

Chapter Ten

A Light to the Nations

FROM the beginning God created Israel to be a missionary people—His ambassadors in the earth. He intended from the start for them to be a light to the nations; a spiritual beacon shining in the darkness of the world, pointing the way to God. The children of Israel were to be God's servants and priests, His messengers of truth and righteousness. The Bible, and the Book of Isaiah in particular, is full of references to this missionary purpose.

> *I am the Lord, I have called you in righteousness, I will also hold you by the hand and watch over you, and I will appoint you as a covenant to the people, as a light to the nations* (Isaiah 42:6).

> *"You are My witnesses," declares the Lord, "and My servant whom I have chosen"* (Isaiah 43:10a).

God's original intention was that, after calling out and raising up the nation of Israel, He would give them His law and teach them how to love, serve, honor, and obey Him. As they did this God would bless them: They would prosper, their crops would not fail, there would be no drought, they would not suffer any of the diseases that plagued other nations, and they would defeat any enemies who came against them. Then, as the people of other nations saw the blessedness of Israel, they would be drawn to ask, "What is it about you that is different? What do you have that we don't that you should be so favored?" This would open the door for Israel to tell about their wonderful God and His great love and saving power. (Ultimately, of course, God's purpose in Israel was to bring the Messiah into the world, the sinless Son of God whose death would take away the sins of the world.)

The Israelites' blessedness and the fulfillment of their call as a light to the nations were conditional upon their obedience to God. Unfortunately, the people of Israel by and large failed to fulfill their call. Instead of becoming a missionary nation they became exclusive, hoarding God's blessings and exploiting their "status" as God's special, chosen people. In disobedience they turned away from God. Eventually they lost His blessings, and their nation was destroyed.

This does not mean, however, that God's purpose has changed; He still desires to reach the nations. He has raised up the Church to carry out what Israel failed to do.[1] Jesus said, "You are the light of the world....Let your light shine before men in such a way that they may see your good works, and glorify your Father who is in heaven" (Mt. 5:14a,16).

Later, before He ascended into Heaven, Jesus laid upon His disciples these charges: "Go therefore and make disciples of all the nations, baptizing them in the name of the Father and the Son and the Holy Spirit, teaching them to observe all that I commanded you" (Mt. 28:19-20a), and "You shall receive power when the Holy Spirit has come upon you; and you shall be My witnesses both in Jerusalem, and in all Judea and Samaria, and even to the remotest part of the earth" (Acts 1:8).

God's purpose is to reach the nations, and this purpose is linked to His concern for His glory.

UNTIL GOD'S GLORY FILLS THE EARTH

Our God is a God of divine objective. He is always at work. A divine purpose is behind His every action. He does not simply sit back in Heaven passively watching what goes on below; God is actively engaged in the affairs of this world. Throughout history God has always chosen people to be involved with Him in carrying out His purpose. First there was Abraham, then Moses and the nation of Israel, then Jesus, and finally, the Church. What God purposes to do He will accomplish. Nothing can divert or defeat His plan.

I am God, and there is no other; I am God, and there is no one like Me...My purpose will be established, and I will accomplish all My good pleasure (Isaiah 46:9b-10).

Not only is God's purpose undefeatable, it is also unchanging.

In the same way God, desiring even more to show to the heirs of the promise the unchangeableness of His purpose, interposed with an oath, in order that by two unchangeable things, in which it is impossible for God to lie, we may have strong encouragement, we who have fled for refuge in laying hold of the hope set before us (Hebrews 6:17-18).

Although God's purpose never changes, the means He uses to accomplish it does. God uses people as His instruments of purpose, and each generation calls for new and different methods. Though the instruments change and the methods vary, God's purpose always remains the same.

So what is God's purpose? Ultimately, His purpose is to fill the earth with His glory. God said to Moses, "But indeed, as I live, all the earth will be filled with the glory of the Lord" (Num. 14:21). The prophet Habakkuk wrote, "For the earth will be filled with the knowledge of the glory of the Lord, as the waters cover the sea" (Hab. 2:14).

There is so much that could be said about the glory of God that scores of books could be written (and probably have been) without exhausting the subject. Let me simply say here that I believe, essentially, the glory of God is His nature and character revealed. God is very jealous of His glory. As our Father, He freely gives us all things according to His will. We share in His Kingdom, but the one thing He will not share is His glory. "I am the Lord, that is My name; I will not give My glory to another, nor My praise to graven images" (Is. 42:8). "For My own sake, for My own sake, I will act; for how can My name be profaned? And My glory I will not give to another" (Is. 48:11).

We live in an idolatrous world that routinely profanes God's name. However, all history is progressing toward a day when that will change. The day is coming when everyone will acknowledge His glory. The focal point will be Jesus Christ who, after...

> *...becoming obedient to the point of death, even death on a cross...God highly exalted Him, and bestowed on Him the name which is above every name, that at the name of Jesus every knee should bow, of those who are in heaven, and on earth, and under the earth, and that every tongue should confess that Jesus Christ is Lord, to the glory of God the Father* (Philippians 2:8b-11).

Jesus Christ was the perfect manifestation of the glory of God, revealing the divine character and nature in everything He said and did. Speaking of Christ, Paul wrote, "For in Him all the fulness of Deity dwells in bodily form" (Col. 2:9). Jesus expressed the very likeness, image, love, grace, mercy, forgiveness, and compassion of God. He manifested God's glory to His disciples so that He might in turn manifest it in them and then through them to the world. God's glory will fill the earth as He reveals His nature and character in and through His people.

THE PARABLE OF JONAH

The Book of Jonah is the "missionary book" of the Old Testament. Although it is the true story of one wayward Jewish prophet, it is also a parable illustrating God's purpose for the nation of Israel. Just as God's purpose for Israel was to reach the nations, so He called Jonah to go to Nineveh, the capital of Assyria, a Gentile nation and traditional enemy of Israel. Jonah rebelled, of course, and took off in the opposite direction. He tried to flee as far away as he could from God's calling on his life.

Jonah couldn't escape from God, however, and was thrown into the sea where God had prepared a great fish to swallow him. Jonah spent three days in "captivity" in the belly of the fish, during which time he prayed, repented, renewed his commitment to God, and promised to obey Him. The fish spit Jonah out onto dry ground, and he finally got on his way to Nineveh. For 40 days he preached God's judgment on the city for its sin. The Ninevites repented and God relented. A disgruntled Jonah complained that God had not carried out the promised judgment—after all, these were hated enemies of Israel. God gently reminded Jonah that He loves and has compassion for all people, Jew or Gentile.

When Israel failed repeatedly to obey God, even turning away from Him to follow after other gods, He sent them into a 70-year captivity in Babylon. The years of captivity cured Israel's idolatrous spirit, and after God restored them to their homeland, they never again as a nation followed idols (at least not the graven image kind). However, they still had trouble comprehending God's love and mercy toward the Gentiles.

Jeremiah described Israel's captivity in terms strongly reminiscent of Jonah's story. In this passage Israel says,

> *Nebuchadnezzar king of Babylon has devoured me and crushed me, he has set me down like an empty vessel; he has swallowed me like a monster, he has filled his stomach with my delicacies; he has washed me away* (Jeremiah 51:34).

The Lord replies,

> *And I shall punish Bel in Babylon, and I shall make what he has swallowed come out of his mouth; and the nations will no longer stream to him. Even the wall of Babylon has fallen down! Come forth from her midst, My people, and each of you save yourselves from the fierce anger of the Lord* (Jeremiah 51:44-45).

In other words, Babylon was like a huge fish that swallowed up the nation of Israel for 70 years, until they learned their lesson. Then God restored them, bringing them out of Babylon's "mouth" and leading them back to their own land.

So Jonah is symbolic of Israel. Like Jonah, Israel rebelled. They wanted the blessings of God but were unwilling to accept the responsibility that came with them. We need to be careful because we have the same problem in the Church today. We want all the blessings of God but none of the responsibility that goes with them. We want the refreshing of the "river" but not the discipline of the race. Let us heed the lessons of Jonah and Israel—lest we reap the same results.

A KINGDOM OF PRIESTS

Let's go back to the Israelites' first deliverance from captivity. Shortly after leaving Egypt, God gave Moses some specific directions concerning His purpose for Israel.

> *"You yourselves have seen what I did to the Egyptians, and how I bore you on eagles' wings, and brought you to Myself. Now then, if you will indeed obey My voice and keep My covenant, then you shall be My own possession among all the peoples, for all the earth is Mine; and you shall be to Me a kingdom of priests and a holy nation." These are the words that you shall speak to the sons of Israel* (Exodus 19:4-6).

God called Israel to be "a kingdom of priests and a holy nation," a people set apart exclusively for God. Now what does that mean? What is the function of a priest? Obviously, the highest function of a priest is to minister to God, but he also ministers to the people on God's behalf. In many ways, a priest is a mediator, a go-between for the people in their relationship with God.

Every priest has a parish, a group of people or a geographical district for which he has pastoral responsibility. But what about an entire nation of priests? What is their parish? Most biblical scholars agree that if Israel was called as a kingdom of priests, then their parish was all the other nations of the earth. In God's original design, theirs was a universal priesthood with the function of leading the nations of the earth to worship and serve the one true living and holy God.

The Church today has the same priestly function with relation to the world. One of the major doctrines restored to the Church through the Protestant Reformation was the priesthood of the believer. Every believer is equally a priest before God. This means that no mediator stands between us and God other than Christ Himself. We have direct and ready access to the

Father. Being a priest also means that we are responsible for bearing witness of Christ to others who need God's saving grace.

Peter wrote that, as priests, our service to God is that of offering up spiritual sacrifices. These include the sacrifice of praise and thanksgiving. Praise and thanksgiving, I believe, are the natural outflow of the first and basic sacrifice—the surrender of our bodies to God as living sacrifices. Only when God has Lordship over our lives can He begin to place His purpose and burden upon us.

Paul understood this priestly function of the believer. He told the Romans that because of God's grace toward him, he was "a minister of Christ Jesus to the Gentiles, ministering as a priest the gospel of God, that my offering of the Gentiles might become acceptable, sanctified by the Holy Spirit" (Rom. 15:16). This is the only instance Paul used the word *priest* in reference to Christian life and ministry.

Paul was a priest; the offering he was bringing to God was Gentile converts, because his call from God was to carry the gospel to the Gentile world. Paul, a Jew, was individually fulfilling the call that God had given to the entire Jewish nation centuries before.

THE UNFRUITFUL VINEYARD

Chapter 5 of Isaiah contains a sad parable about Israel.

Let me sing now for my well-beloved a song of my beloved concerning His vineyard. My well-beloved had a vineyard on a fertile hill. And He dug it all around, removed its stones, and planted it with the choicest vine. And He built a tower in the middle of it, and hewed out a wine vat in it; then He expected it to produce good grapes, but it produced only worthless ones. "And now, O inhabitants of Jerusalem and men of Judah, judge between Me and My vineyard. What more was there to do for My vineyard that I have not done in it? Why, when I expected it to produce good grapes did it produce worthless ones? So now let Me tell you what I am going to do to My vineyard: I will remove its hedge and it will be consumed; I will break down its wall and it will become trampled ground" (Isaiah 5:1-5).

The "well-beloved" is God; the vineyard is Israel. God lavished His love and care on them, giving them every advantage, every opportunity, every reason, and every privilege to grow and be fruitful. Can't you hear the disappointment in God's voice when He asks, "What more was there to do for My vineyard that I have not done in it? Why, when I expected it to produce good grapes did it produce worthless ones?" Despite the fact that they had everything going for them, Israel failed to produce the spiritual fruit God was looking for. They failed to fulfill His purpose and failed to realize His hopes and plans for them. Therefore, God removed His hedge of protection from around them.

Centuries later Jesus referred to this sad tale in a parable He taught in the temple in Jerusalem. Among His listeners were the chief priests and elders, the spiritual leaders of the Jews. "Listen to another parable. There was a landowner who planted a vineyard and put a wall around it and dug a wine press in it, and built a tower, and rented it out to vine-growers, and went on a journey. And when the harvest time approached, he sent his slaves to the vine-growers to receive his produce" (Mt. 21:33-34). The vine-growers, however, beat one slave, killed another, and stoned a third. A second, larger contingent of slaves met the same treatment. Finally, the landowner sent his son, but the vine-growers killed him also.

> *Therefore when the owner of the vineyard comes, what will he do to those vine-growers? They said to Him, "He will bring those wretches to a wretched end, and will rent out the vineyard to other vine-growers, who will pay him the proceeds at the proper seasons." Jesus said to them, "Did you never read in the Scriptures, 'The stone which the builders rejected, this became the chief corner stone; this came about from the Lord, and it is marvelous in our eyes'? Therefore I say to you, the kingdom of God will be taken away from you, and be given to a nation producing the fruit of it"* (Matthew 21:40-43).

In this parable the landowner of course is God, the vineyard is Israel, and the vine-growers are the priests and elders of the people. The slaves who were so mistreated represent the prophets of God, while the landowner's son represents Jesus Himself.

Now, the only purpose of a vine is to produce grapes; it is useless for anything else. Apart from the harvest of fruit it produces, a vine has no function. One reason that Israel (the vineyard) was unfruitful was because the priests and elders (the vine-growers) were unfaithful. Their rebellion led the nation into disobedience and fruitlessness.

The prophets (the slaves) were persecuted because they understood the mind of God for the nation of Israel and tried to get the people to repent and return to Him. The prophets knew that the people of Israel had a mandate to be God's servants and a light to the nations. Instead, the Israelites came to despise other nations and got caught up in their own little self-centered world. In so doing, they also despised the calling God had placed on them. They desired God's blessings and privileges, but they wanted nothing to do with His greater purpose.

When Jesus asked the chief priests and elders what the landowner should do, they fell into His carefully laid trap. By their own lips, they pronounced God's judgment upon themselves. The vineyard would be taken from the vine-growers, they would be punished, and the vineyard rented out to other vine-growers who would be faithful in producing fruit.

Jesus made it clear. "The kingdom of God will be taken away from you, and be given to a nation producing the fruit of it." Israel was unfruitful, so God would raise up another nation that would be fruitful.

A ROYAL PRIESTHOOD

Who is this other nation? Simon Peter gives us the answer. Writing to the Christian believers scattered across Asia Minor, he says,

But you are a chosen race, a royal priesthood, a holy nation, a people for God's own possession, that you may proclaim the excellencies of Him who has called you out of darkness into His marvelous light; for you once were not a people, but now you are the people of God; you had not received mercy, but now you have received mercy (1 Peter 2:9-10).

"A chosen race, a royal priesthood, a holy nation"—does any of that sound familiar? God's call to the Church is the same call He gave to the nation of Israel: to "proclaim the excellencies" of God to the world. Once Israel had not been a nation, but God raised them up into a people of His possession. Likewise the Gentiles, who by this time greatly outnumbered the Jews in the ranks of the Church, "once were not a people"; now they were God's people, having received His mercy. God has always been in the business of raising up a people for His own possession—a body of persons who will obey His commands and do His will.

Remember that in the natural order there is no such thing as royalty in the priesthood; kings are kings and priests are priests. In the divine order, however, Christ not only is King of kings but also a priest forever after the order of Melchizedek. The risen Christ is the "firstfruits" of all who are alive in God (see 1 Cor. 15:20). All of us, then, who are children of God in Christ are kings by birth and priests by calling.

As believers, we are the spiritual seed of Abraham. Abraham was the "father" of the Jews, but it was a spiritual parentage more than it was a physical one. True children of Abraham are children of faith, not flesh. Paul wrote, "For he is not a Jew who is one outwardly; neither is circumcision that which is outward in the flesh. But he is a Jew who is one inwardly; and circumcision is that which is of the heart, by the Spirit, not by the letter; and his praise is not from men, but from God" (Rom. 2:28-29). It was Abraham's faith that made him right with God. "Then he believed in the Lord; and He reckoned it to him as righteousness" (Gen. 15:6). Likewise, we are "justified by faith, [and] have peace with God through our Lord Jesus Christ" (Rom. 5:1).

The ultimate purpose of God's covenant with Abraham was to bless the world and bring to it the light and knowledge of God. As Abraham's spiritual children, we are part of that covenant. The same call that was on Abraham is on us as well. Israel's mandate to be a light to the nations is our mandate also.

CHRIST, THE ETERNAL SEED

Indeed, we are Abraham's spiritual offspring and children of the covenant. However, there is another descendant of Abraham to whom the covenant points. In fact, He is the focal point of the entire witness of Scripture: our Savior, Jesus Christ. After Abraham had demonstrated his faith and trust in God by not withholding Isaac, the Lord reaffirmed His promise:

By Myself I have sworn, declares the Lord, because you have done this thing, and have not withheld your son, your only son, indeed I will greatly bless you, and I will greatly multiply your seed as the stars of the heavens, and as the sand which is on the seashore; and your seed shall possess the gate of their enemies. And in your seed all the nations of the earth shall be blessed, because you have obeyed My voice (Genesis 22:16-18).

In Galatians 3 Paul comments on Abraham and his "seed":

Now the promises were spoken to Abraham and to his seed. He does not say, "And to seeds," as referring to many, but rather to one, "And to your seed," that is, Christ (Galatians 3:16).

What Paul means here is that Jesus Christ was the ultimate fulfillment of God's promise to Abraham. Christ Himself was the "seed" through whom the whole earth would be blessed. Everything in the Abrahamic covenant, everything in the Scriptures, everything about God's plans and dealings with Israel—all points to Christ. He is the focal point, the nexus, of human history and of God's redemptive plan for the human race. In Christ, everything comes together.

Luke brings out this point in the last chapter of his Gospel. After His resurrection Jesus met two of His followers on the road to Emmaus, but they failed to recognize Him. The three of them talked about what had just happened in Jerusalem (Jesus' crucifixion), as well as the report from some that Jesus had risen. The two walking with Jesus expressed their doubts about all this. Finally, Jesus says to them, " 'O foolish men and slow of heart to believe in all that the prophets have spoken! Was it not necessary for the Christ to suffer these things and to enter into His glory?' And beginning with Moses and with all the prophets, He explained to them the things concerning Himself in all the Scriptures" (Lk. 24:25-27). Later that same day Jesus appeared in the midst of His disciples and said, "These are My words which I spoke to you while I was still with you, that all things which are written about Me in the Law of Moses and the Prophets and the Psalms must be fulfilled" (Lk. 24:44).

So there is a concise summary of the theme of the entire Old Testament: The Law, the Prophets, and the Psalms all point to Christ. He is the One whom God had promised to raise up to bless all the nations of the earth.

ROYAL HEIRS

Paul is not finished with his discussion of Christ as the seed of Abraham, however. He says that because all believers are spiritual children of Abraham, we too are included in God's covenant plan!

For you are all sons of God through faith in Christ Jesus. For all of you who were baptized into Christ have clothed yourselves with Christ. There is neither Jew nor Greek, there is neither slave nor free man, there is neither male nor female; for you are all one in Christ Jesus. And if you belong to Christ, then you are Abraham's offspring, heirs according to promise (Galatians 3:26-29).

In other words, the moment you and I accept Christ, we come into the Body of Christ, the Church. In Christ all the dividers come down. Spiritually speaking, there is no distinction between Jew and Gentile, male and female, socioeconomic levels, or class standing. We are all one in Christ.

If we are in Christ, we are "Abraham's offspring, heirs according to promise." An heir, obviously, is someone who receives an inheritance. We have inherited the promise God gave to Abraham. As his spiritual offspring, we are heirs to his spiritual legacy of faith. The proof of our inheritance— the down payment, so to speak—is the Holy Spirit living in us. As Paul wrote to the Romans, "The Spirit Himself bears witness with our spirit that we are children of God, and if children, heirs also, heirs of God and fellow heirs with Christ, if indeed we suffer with Him in order that we may also be glorified with Him" (Rom. 8:16-17).

We are fellow heirs with Christ; we are heirs to all the blessings, abundance, and riches of the Kingdom of Heaven. However, Paul also speaks of suffering with Christ in order to be glorified with Him. As heirs of God we have high *privileges*; as fellow heirs with Christ we have heavy *responsibilities*. Privilege and responsibility go together. Israel's downfall was that they tried to separate the two. It won't work. By inheriting the blessings of the covenant we also inherit the responsibilities of the covenant.

The mandate is ours. God still desires to reach the nations, and He has chosen us to carry the gospel to the world. He has blessed us with great privileges and advantages and has equipped us for the task. The question we must ask ourselves is, "Will we?" Israel said no and a generation died in the wilderness. What about us? Are we ready to take up the mantle of the call of God? Are we prepared to move from *privilege* to *purpose*?

ENDNOTES

1. The author does not have time here to elaborate on Israel's future role in God's pupose.

Chapter Eleven

Victims or Victors

REVIVAL FIRES

O NE danger the Church faces during a season of revival is how easily the spiritual passion that is aroused can cross over the line into fleshly excess and worldly indulgence. This is possible because true revival heightens and reinvigorates every aspect of a person's life—mind, body, spirit, and emotions. As human beings, we were created as a unit—body, mind, and spirit—and what affects one part also affects the others to some degree. Think about it. If we become physically ill, it affects us emotionally as well. If our spiritual sensitivity is heightened, we are usually sharper mentally.

In other words, when we are "turned on" spiritually, we also can be "turned on" physically and every other way. There is a tendency, even in the midst of revival, not only for our spiritual passions to be aroused by the freedom in worship with dancing, singing, shouting, laughing, crying, and such, but also for our sexual passions to become aroused. For example, if an attractive young woman is in a service praising the Lord with beautiful, Spirit-inspired dancing, some young men in the congregation (as well as some who are not so young) may begin to look beyond the praise and worship aspect of her dancing and become sexually aroused by her body and physical movements. This can happen even if they have been touched and renewed by the Spirit, because all their senses and sensibilities have been heightened as well. Believe it or not, but it is possible to fall into fleshly lust and worldly desire even in a revival meeting! Satan is always watching for opportunities to trip up unwary believers.

For this reason it is very important to learn to exercise strict self-control and restraint in all things, as Paul did. He was determined not to let anything of the world or the flesh trip him up and cause him to fall, and thereby fail to finish the race. His exhortation to Timothy applies to us as well: "Now flee from youthful lusts, and pursue righteousness, faith, love and peace, with those who call on the Lord from a pure heart" (2 Tim. 2:22).

This is what was behind Israel's downfall in the wilderness. *In spite* of God's powerful presence, *in spite of* all their great privileges and advantages, they gave in to their fleshly lusts and passions and so fell into greed, idolatry, immorality, rebellion, and grumbling. Their lack of self-control caused them to miss being involved with God in accomplishing His divine and redemptive purpose in the world.

We are no different; the same temptations that destroyed Israel in the wilderness threaten us today, *especially* during a season of revival. This is why we must be so careful. The key to victory is to "flee youthful lusts, and pursue righteousness, faith, love, and peace." It is to heed Paul's warning, "Therefore let him who thinks he stands take heed lest he fall" (1 Cor. 10:12). That warning comes with an encouragement, however: "No temptation has overtaken you but such as is common to man; and God is faithful, who will not allow you to be tempted beyond what you are able, but with the temptation will provide the way of escape also, that you may be able to endure it" (1 Cor. 10:13). Paul's words to us are, "Control yourselves. Get your eyes fixed firmly on the goal and go for the gold! Press forward for the prize! Run in such a way as to win. Finish the race!"

FINISHING THE RACE

What does it mean to finish the race? Essentially, I believe finishing the race means having a peace in your spirit that you have done everything God asked you to do. In other words, finishing the race means living in full obedience to the will of God. This will work itself out differently for each person. For one it may mean laboring faithfully for 30 years as the shepherd of a church that never grows beyond 12 members, living far from the limelight or any public recognition. For another it may mean conducting an international ministry that touches the lives of hundreds of thousands of people. For most of us it probably means simply living faithfully day in and day out on the job, at home, in the church, and in the community, seeking daily to hear and follow the voice of the Lord.

The important thing is not how much we have but how we use what God has given to us. Remember Jesus' parable of the talents? Matthew 25:14-30 recounts how a master, before leaving on a journey, called three of his slaves. He gave five talents to one, two talents to another, and one talent to the third. The first two immediately put their talents to work and doubled their money. The third slave did nothing except bury his master's money. Upon the master's return, the first two slaves were praised and rewarded for their faithfulness and fruitfulness and were ushered into the joy of their master. The unfaithful and unfruitful slave, however, was cast out into the "outer darkness." We all have different giftings and capabilities, and if we are one-talent people, God will not place upon us a five-talent responsibility. He will, however, hold us accountable for the one talent He entrusted to us.

By the world's standards Jesus would have been considered a failure during His lifetime. All He had to show for three years of ministry was a handful of followers and a criminal's death as an enemy of the state. He left no family, no estate, no monuments or statues. Yet, in truth, Jesus was thoroughly and completely successful because He fulfilled everything His Father gave Him to do. Jesus completed His race, giving His victory cry from the cross: "It is finished!"

At the end of his life Paul had the satisfaction of heart and the peace of spirit that he had completed his race.

> For I am already being poured out as a drink offering, and the time of my departure has come. I have fought the good fight, I have finished the course, I have kept the faith; in the future there is laid up for me the crown of righteousness, which the Lord, the righteous Judge, will award to me on that day; and not only to me, but also to all who have loved His appearing (2 Timothy 4:6-8).

Finishing the race also means *winning*. In the spiritual race, everyone who finishes wins. We are not competing against one another; we simply are striving to live each day under the authority and Lordship of Christ and to walk in His power and grace. Finishing the race means laying aside "every encumbrance, and the sin which so easily entangles us, and let us run with endurance the race that is set before us, fixing our eyes on Jesus, the author and perfecter of faith, who for the joy set before Him endured the cross, despising the shame, and has sat down at the right hand of the throne of God" (Heb. 12:1a-2).

If finishing the race means winning, then winning means never, ever quitting, no matter what the obstacles or how impossible the race seems.

During the marathon race of the 1968 summer Olympic Games in Mexico City, John Stephen Akhwari, the runner representing the African nation of Tanzania, took a painful fall on the crowded streets of the city and gashed his leg badly. Pausing only long enough to have his wound bandaged, the athlete gamely struggled on, pain accompanying every stride. He finally limped into the Olympic stadium more than an hour after the first-place winner had crossed the finish line and all but the most stalwart fans and spectators had left. When asked why he continued to run when he had such a painful injury and was so hopelessly far behind, Akhwari replied, "My country did not send me 7,000 miles to start the race. They sent me to finish!"

That's the spirit of a winner!

God is pouring out His blessings and refreshing on His Church once again. The "river" *is* here. Yet we must be careful that we do not go the way of Israel, who drank from the river and died in the wilderness. There is more to the river than just refreshing. The Lord is calling us to move from privilege to purpose; He is calling us to press forward from the refreshing of the river to the discipline of the race. We must pour ourselves out to reach a world in need of Christ. We are to be artesian springs from whose "innermost being shall flow rivers of living water" (Jn. 7:38) Let us commit ourselves to the task and, like Paul, "press on toward the goal for the prize of the upward call of God in Christ Jesus" (Phil. 3:14). Let us be careful that we don't drink from the river and then die with our running shoes on. God has blessed us with great privilege, but He has called us to great responsibility. Let's fix our eyes on the goal, run in such a way as to win, and press ahead together into the greater purpose of God!

Also by
David Ravenhill

FOR GOD'S SAKE GROW UP!

by David Ravenhill.
It's time to grow up...so that we can fulfill God's purposes for us and for our generation! For too long we've been spiritual children clinging to our mother's leg, refusing to go to school on the first day. It's time to put away childish things and mature in the things of God—there is a world that needs to be won to Christ!
ISBN 1-56043-299-3

For those interested in contacting the author for speaking engagements write to:

David Ravenhill
Spikenard Ministries Ltd.
16858 Hwy 110 North
Lindale, TX   75771

Or call:
903-882-3942

Or FAX:
903-882-3740

Other
Destiny Image titles
you will enjoy reading

THE GOD CHASERS (National best-selling book)
by Tommy Tenney.
There are those so hungry, so desperate for His presence, that they become consumed with finding Him. Their longing for Him moves them to do what they would otherwise never do: Chase God. But what does it really mean to chase God? Can He be "caught"? Is there an end to the thirsting of man's soul for Him? Meet Tommy Tenney—God chaser. Join him in his search for God. Follow him as he ignores the maze of religious tradition and finds himself, not chasing God, but to his utter amazement, caught by the One he had chased.
ISBN 0-7684-2016-4

GOD CHASERS DAILY MEDITATION & PERSONAL JOURNAL
by Tommy Tenney.
ISBN 0-7684-2040-7

GOD'S FAVORITE HOUSE (National best-selling book)
by Tommy Tenney.
The burning desire of your heart can be fulfilled. God is looking for people just like you. He is a Lover in search of a people who will love Him in return. He is far more interested in you than He is interested in a building. He would hush all of Heaven's hosts to listen to your voice raised in heartfelt love songs to Him. This book will show you how to build a house of worship within, fulfilling your heart's desire and His!
ISBN 0-7684-2043-1

THE LOST PASSIONS OF JESUS
by Donald L. Milam, Jr.
What motivated Jesus to pursue the cross? What inner strength kept His feet on the path laid before Him? Time and tradition have muted the Church's knowledge of the passions that burned in Jesus' heart, but if we want to—if we dare to—we can still seek those same passions. Learn from a close look at Jesus' own life and words and from the writings of other dedicated followers the passions that enflamed the Son of God and changed the world forever!
ISBN 0-9677402-0-7

AN INVITATION TO FRIENDSHIP:
From the Father's Heart, Volume 2
by Charles Slagle.
Our God is a Father whose heart longs for His children to sit and talk with Him in fellowship and oneness. This second volume of intimate letters from the Father to you, His child, reveals His passion, dreams, and love for you. As you read them, you will find yourself drawn ever closer within the circle of His embrace. The touch of His presence will change your life forever!
ISBN 0-7684-2013-X

Available at your local Christian bookstore.

Internet: http://www.reapernet.com

Other
*Destiny Image **titles***
you will enjoy reading

Other
*Destiny Image **titles***
you will enjoy reading

THE POWER OF BROKENNESS
by Don Nori.
Accepting Brokenness is a must for becoming a true vessel of the Lord, and is a stepping-stone to revival in our hearts, our homes, and our churches. Brokenness alone brings us to the wonderful revelation of how deep and great our Lord's mercy really is. Join this companion who leads us through the darkest of nights. Discover the *Power of Brokenness*.
ISBN 1-56043-178-4

HIS MANIFEST PRESENCE
by Don Nori.
This is a passionate look at God's desire for a people with whom He can have intimate fellowship. Not simply a book on worship, it faces our triumphs as well as our sorrows in relation to God's plan for a dwelling place that is splendid in holiness and love.
ISBN 0-914903-48-9
Also available in Spanish.
ISBN 1-56043-079-6

SECRETS OF THE MOST HOLY PLACE
by Don Nori.
Here is a prophetic parable you will read again and again. The winds of God are blowing, drawing you to His Life within the Veil of the Most Holy Place. There you begin to see as you experience a depth of relationship your heart has yearned for. This book is a living, dynamic experience with God!
ISBN 1-56043-076-1

ENCOUNTERING THE PRESENCE
by Colin Urquhart.
What is it about Jesus that, when we encounter Him, we are changed? When we encounter the Presence, we encounter the Truth, because Jesus is the Truth. Here Colin Urquhart, best-selling author and pastor in Sussex, England, explains how the Truth changes facts. Do you desire to become more like Jesus? The Truth will set you free!
ISBN 0-7684-2018-0

Available at your local Christian bookstore.

Internet: http://www.reapernet.com

Other
Destiny Image titles
you will enjoy reading

HIDDEN TREASURES OF THE HEART
by Donald Downing.
What is hidden in your heart? Your heart is the key to life—both natural and spiritual. If you aren't careful with your heart, you run the risk of becoming vulnerable to the attacks of the enemy. This book explains the changes you need to make to ensure that your commitment to God is from the heart and encourages you to make those changes. Don't miss out on the greatest blessing of all—a clean heart!
ISBN 1-56043-315-9

THE LOST ART OF INTERCESSION
by Jim W. Goll.
Finally there is something that really explains what is happening to so many folk in the Body of Christ. What does it mean to carry the burden of the Lord? Where is it in Scripture and in history? Why do I feel as though God is groaning within me? No, you are not crazy; God is restoring genuine intercessory prayer in the hearts of those who are open to respond to His burden and His passion.
ISBN 1-56043-697-2

THE HIDDEN POWER OF PRAYER AND FASTING
by Mahesh Chavda.
The praying believer is the confident believer. But the fasting believer is the overcoming believer. This is the believer who changes the circumstances and the world around him. He is the one who experiences the supernatural power of the risen Lord in his everyday life. An international evangelist and the senior pastor of All Nations Church in Charlotte, North Carolina, Mahesh Chavda has seen firsthand the power of God released through a lifestyle of prayer and fasting. Here he shares from decades of personal experience and scriptural study principles and practical tips about fasting and praying. This book will inspire you to tap into God's power and change your life, your city, and your nation!
ISBN 0-7684-2017-2

THE RELEASE OF THE HUMAN SPIRIT
by Frank Houston.
Your relationship and walk with the Lord will only go as deep as your spirit is free. Many things "contain" people and keep them in a box—old traditions, wrong thinking, religious mind-sets, emotional hurts, bitterness—the list is endless. A New Zealander by birth and a naturalized Australian citizen, Frank Houston has been jumping out of those "boxes" all his life. For more than 50 years he has been busy living in revival and fulfilling his God-given destiny, regardless of what other people—or even himself—think! In this book you'll discover what it takes to "break out" and find release in the fullness of your Lord. The joy and fulfillment that you will experience will catapult you into a greater and fuller level of living!
ISBN 0-7684-2019-9

Available at your local Christian bookstore.

Internet: http://www.reapernet.com

Other
Destiny Image titles
you will enjoy reading

THE COSTLY ANOINTING
by Lori Wilke.
In this book, teacher and prophetic songwriter Lori Wilke boldly reveals God's requirements for being entrusted with an awesome power and authority. She speaks directly
from God's heart to your heart concerning the most costly anointing. This is a word that
will change your life!
ISBN 1-56043-051-6

A HEART FOR GOD
by Charles P. Schmitt.
This powerful book will send you on a 31-day journey with David from brokenness
to wholeness. Few men come to God with as many millstones around their necks as
David did. Nevertheless, David pressed beyond adversity, sin, and failure into the
very forgiveness and deliverance of God. The life of David will bring hope to those
bound by generational curses, those born in sin, and those raised in shame. David's
life will inspire faith in the hearts of the dysfunctional, the failure-ridden, and the
fallen!
ISBN 1-56043-157-1

REQUIREMENTS FOR GREATNESS
by Lori Wilke.
Everyone longs for greatness, but do we know what God's requirements are? In this
life-changing message, Lori Wilke shows how Jesus exemplified true greatness, and
how we must take on His attributes of justice, mercy, and humility to attain that
greatness in His Kingdom.
ISBN 1-56043-152-0

THE ASCENDED LIFE
by Bernita J. Conway.
A believer does not need to wait until Heaven to experience an intimate relationship
with the Lord. When you are born again, your life becomes His, and He pours His life
into yours. Here Bernita Conway explains from personal study and experience the
truth of "abiding in the Vine," the Lord Jesus Christ. When you grasp this understanding and begin to walk in it, it will change your whole life and relationship with
your heavenly Father!
ISBN 1-56043-337-X

Available at your local Christian bookstore.
Internet: http://www.reapernet.com

Other
Destiny Image titles
you will enjoy reading

FATHER, FORGIVE US!

by Jim W. Goll.

What is holding back a worldwide "great awakening"? What hinders the Church all over the world from rising up and bringing in the greatest harvest ever known? The answer is simple: sin! God is calling Christians today to take up the mantle of identificational intercession and repent for the sins of the present and past; for the sins of our fathers; for the sins of the nations. Will you heed the call? This book shows you how!
ISBN 0-7684-2025-3

FLOODS UPON DRY GROUND

by Charles P. Schmitt.

Do you really know the history of the Church through the ages? This book may surprise you! Charles P. Schmitt, pastor of Immanuel's Church in the Washington D.C. area, gives an inspiring and thought-provoking history of the Church from a charismatic perspective. History is not finished yet, and neither is God! Rediscover your roots and learn how the current rivers of renewal and revival fit into God's great plan for this world.
ISBN 0-7684-2012-1

DIGGING THE WELLS OF REVIVAL

by Lou Engle.

Did you know that just beneath your feet are deep wells of revival? God is calling us today to unstop the wells and reclaim the spiritual inheritance of our nation, declares Lou Engle. As part of the pastoral staff at Harvest Rock Church and founder of its "24-Hour House of Prayer," he has experienced firsthand the importance of knowing and praying over our spiritual heritage. Let's renew covenant with God, reclaim our glorious roots, and believe for the greatest revival the world has ever known!
ISBN 0-7684-2015-6

Available at your local Christian bookstore.

Internet: http://www.reapernet.com

Other
*Destiny Image **titles***
you will enjoy reading

THE THRESHOLD OF GLORY
Compiled by Dotty Schmitt.
What does it mean to experience the "glory of God"? How does it come? These women of God have crossed that threshold, and it changed not only their ministries but also their very lives! Here Dotty Schmitt and Sue Ahn, Bonnie Chavda, Pat Chen, Dr. Flo Ellers, Brenda Kilpatrick, and Varle Rollins teach about God's glorious presence and share how it transformed their lives.
ISBN 0-7684-2044-X

ONLY BELIEVE
by Don Stewart.
Who was A.A. Allen, John Dowie, Maria Woodworth-Etter, and William Branham? Who were these and the many other people who picked up the mantle of the healing evangelist in the twentieth century? What was their legacy? Don Stewart, who was mentored by A.A. Allen and had contact with most of his contemporaries in this widespread movement, gives an inside look into their lives and ministries. This incredible, firsthand witness account of the events and people who have shaped our current Christian heritage will astound you with how God takes frail, human vessels, pours out His anointing, and enables them to do mighty exploits for Him!
ISBN 1-56043-340-X

ENCOUNTERS WITH A SUPERNATURAL GOD
by Jim W. and Michal Ann Goll.
The Golls know that angels are real. They have firsthand experience with supernatural angelic encounters. In this book you'll read and learn about angels and supernatural manifestations of God's Presence—and the real encounters that both Jim and Michal Ann have had! As the founders of Ministry to the Nations and speakers and teachers, they share that God wants to be intimate friends with His people. Go on an adventure with the Golls and find out if God has a supernatural encounter for you!
ISBN 1-56043-199-7

Available at your local Christian bookstore.
Internet: http://www.reapernet.com

Other
Destiny Image ***titles***
you will enjoy reading

WOMEN ON THE FRONT LINES
by Michal Ann Goll.
History is filled with ordinary women who have changed the course of their generation. Here Michal Ann Goll, co-founder of Ministry to the Nations with her husband, Jim, shares how her own life was transformed and highlights nine women whose lives will impact yours! Every generation faces the same choices and issues; learn how you, too, can heed the call to courage and impact a generation.
ISBN 0-7684-2020-2

WOMAN: HER PURPOSE, POSITION, AND POWER
by Mary Jean Pidgeon.
When the enemy slipped into the garden, he robbed Eve and all her daughters of their original purpose, position, and power. But today God is bringing these truths back to women. He is setting His daughters free and showing them their value in His Kingdom. Let Mary Jean Pidgeon, a wife, mother, and the Associate Pastor with her husband, Pastor Jack Pidgeon, in Houston, explain a woman's *purpose*, *position*, and *power*.
ISBN 1-56043-330-2

HINDS' FEET ON HIGH PLACES (Women's Devotional)
by Hannah Hurnard.
What can be more exciting than the *Hinds' Feet on High Places* allegory? It is the allegory along with a daily devotional for women by a woman who has proven her walk with the Lord and her writing gift with other inspirational books. Most of these devotions are "quiet time" meditations, ones that will draw you closer to your Lord Jesus. They will help you to understand your own struggles and regain confidence in your walk with the Lord. This allegory with the devotionals will help satisfy the yearning of your heart. He is challenging you to keep saying "yes" to your Lord as He beckons you on in your own journey to the High Places.
ISBN 0-7684-2035-0

Available at your local Christian bookstore.
Internet: http://www.reapernet.com

Other
Destiny Image **titles**
you will enjoy reading

UNDERSTANDING THE DREAMS YOU DREAM
by Ira Milligan.
Have you ever had a dream in which you think God was speaking to you? Here is a practical guide, from the Christian perspective, for understanding the symbolic language of dreams. Deliberately written without technical jargon, this book can be easily understood and used by everyone. Includes a complete dictionary of symbols.
ISBN 1-56043-284-5

DREAMS IN THE SPIRIT, VOL. 1
by Bart Druckenmiller.
We all want to hear the word of the Lord. Nevertheless, many people don't. They limit how God speaks, not recognizing His voice throughout life's experiences, including dreams in the night and "daydreams" born of the Spirit. As a result, our lives lack vision and destiny. This book will introduce you to how God speaks through dreams and visions. It will give you hope that you, too, can learn to hear God's voice in your dreams and fulfill all that He speaks to you.
ISBN 1-56043-346-9

DREAMS: WISDOM WITHIN
by Herman Riffel.
This foremost full-gospel authority discusses how and why God uses dreams. He shows how incorrect assumptions about dreams have caused us to ignore this essential way in which God speaks to His people.
ISBN 1-56043-007-9

DREAM INTERPRETATION
by Herman Riffel.
Many believers read the scriptural accounts of dreams and never think it could happen to them. Today, though, many are realizing that God has never ceased using dreams and visions to guide, instruct, and warn. This book will give you a biblical understanding of dreams that you never had before!
ISBN 1-56043-122-9

Available at your local Christian bookstore.

Internet: http://www.reapernet.com

B6:175

Other
Destiny Image ***titles***
you will enjoy reading

NO MORE SOUR GRAPES
by Don Nori.
Who among us wants our children to be free from the struggles we have had to bear? Who among us wants the lives of our children to be full of victory and love for their Lord? Who among us wants the hard-earned lessons from our lives given freely to our children? All these are not only possible, they are also God's will. You can be one of those who share the excitement and joy of seeing your children step into the destiny God has for them. If you answered "yes" to these questions, the pages of this book are full of hope and help for you and others just like you.
ISBN 0-7684-2037-7

THE BATTLE FOR THE SEED
by Dr. Patricia Morgan.
The dilemma facing young people today is a major concern for all parents. This important book shows God's way to change the condition of the young and advance God's purpose for every nation into the next century.
ISBN 1-56043-099-0

SOLDIERS WITH LITTLE FEET
by Dian Layton.
Every time God pours out His Spirit, the adult generation moves on without its children. Dian pleads with the Church to bring the children into the fullness of God with them and offers practical guidelines for doing so.
ISBN 0-914903-86-1

CHILDREN OF REVIVAL
by Vann Lane.
What do you do with hundreds of children during services that last for hours? At first Pastor Vann Lane thought he would use all his usual "stuff" to entertain the children. The Lord thought differently. In this book you'll read remarkable stories of Brownsville Assembly's 11-year-old leader, the worship band of young musicians, and the 75-member prayer team of children between ages 8 and 12 years old. *Children of Revival* will forever change the way you view the Church's little members.
ISBN 1-56043-699-9

Available at your local Christian bookstore.
Internet: http://www.reapernet.com

B6:176